Planning & Building
PATHS

FRANK GARDNER

MINI · WORKBOOK · SERIES

MEREHURST

CONTENTS

Crazy paving (top left), concrete path (far left) and brick path (left)

This gravel path, flanked by a profusion of colourful plants, works beautifully in an informal setting. Gravel is one of the easiest pathway materials to lay and it is very cost-effective.

Planning your path

Paths are an important part of the garden landscape and provide a low-maintenance surface that enables you to move around your home, or to direct visitors to appropriate entrances. At the same time, paths provide protection for both plants and lawn.

CHOOSING A PATH STYLE

The purpose of your path will play a large part in determining the style of path you choose to construct. A straight path to the main entrance conveys a more formal atmosphere with the front door as the focus; a meandering approach is less formal and invites a leisurely stroll through the garden.

The materials you select are also important. Neat patterns of brick and tile are more formal than the random, mosaic effect of loose material or the rustic feel of timber or natural stone.

Once you have decided on the purpose of your path, choose a style to suit that purpose. The style of path may be influenced by many factors.

• **Direction**. Generally, straight paths have a functional purpose and are used frequently: leading to entrances, exits or to the clothes line. Winding paths tend to blend with the landscape and are more informal, leading perhaps to a garden seat or shady courtyard.

• **Setting**. Choose the style of path to complement either a formal or informal home and garden setting.

Stone, bricks, blocks and tiles are often chosen for paths found in formal settings; materials such as split stone, loose gravel or pebbles, stepping stones or timber are more often seen in informal settings.

• **Architectural style**. Choose a style of path to complement your home. For example, a stepping stone path leading to a summer house looks better than a more formal tiled path.

DECIDING ON DIRECTION

The directions that your paths will take are more important than you think. Paths help to establish the aesthetics of a garden setting.

At this point, it is a good idea to draw up a plan of your house and garden, marking key points such as entry doors, garage, gates, and specific parts of your garden that need connection via a path. Consider also high traffic areas through the garden, to areas such as the garage, pond, clothes line, garden shed, or the need to create paths that make movement easier during bad weather. Once you have done this, you can then decide how you wish to move between each connecting point.

BRICK AND BLOCK PATTERNS

Bricks and blocks make very attractive and durable paths, and the wide variety of colours and textures available makes them a popular choice as a path material. Both can be laid to form many patterns. Some of the more popular styles are shown below.

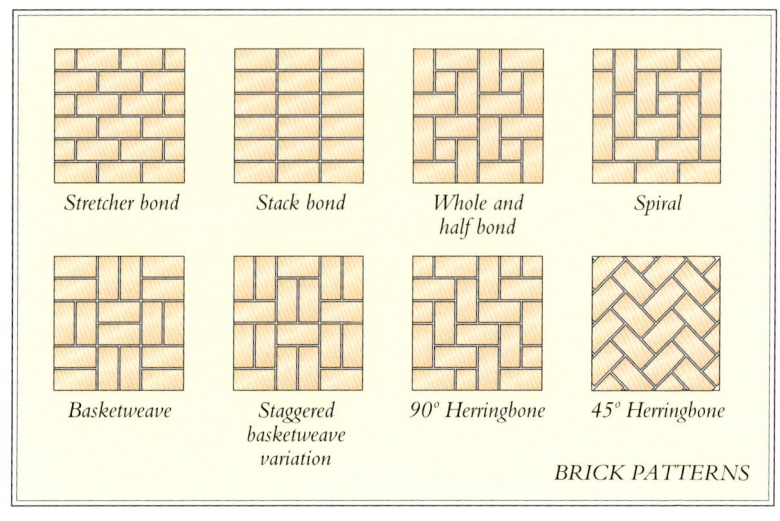

Stretcher bond

Stack bond

Whole and half bond

Spiral

Basketweave

Staggered basketweave variation

90° Herringbone

45° Herringbone

BRICK PATTERNS

STRAIGHT PATHS

If you choose to lay a straight path, try to avoid having it break large areas of space, such as a front lawn, into sections. Instead, run the path down the side boundary and across the front of the house, possibly connecting to the driveway on the other side. Avoid using several short, straight paths, as these tend to break up large areas into small spaces.

CURVED PATHS

Curved paths may vary from a slight curve to a full meander. They soften the landscape and invite leisurely movement along them. Be careful when planning this type of path, as paths that are too curved can make people impatient and they may tend to cut across the lawn or garden.

Curved paths can make a short garden appear longer. This can be achieved by laying a slightly curved path that also decreases slightly in width as it runs up the garden.

A curved path also eliminates the need to remove obstacles, such as favourite trees or garden objects.

In a large, formal landscape setting, a combination of circular paths and radiating straight ones can be used to create an elaborate, interconnecting garden feature.

COPING WITH A SLOPE

Before commencing construction, it is important to examine the degree of slope.

If your site is too steep for ramping, or for visual reasons you want to terrace the area, the solution is the introduction of steps. Do not worry: a slight change of level creates relief in the garden landscape and enhances the setting considerably.

To determine whether you need to construct a ramp or steps, calculate the rate of incline.

• Measure the length of the path.

• If possible, run a string line from one end to the other. Fix the line at ground level at the high end.

• Stretch the string line taut, and check with a spirit level until level.

• At the low end, measure the distance from the string line to the ground to give you the amount of fall over the length of the path.

The rate of incline is a ratio of the fall to the path length (for example, a 1 m fall over a 10 m length of path, gives a rate of incline of 1:10). Ramps may be used when the rate does not exceed 1:10. If the slope is greater than 1:10, it is better to build steps.

At this stage, you should also consider water drainage. Ramped sites pose few problems as ramped paths have natural run-off, but if your site is level, you must put some cross-fall on the path. Cross-fall is necessary to displace water quickly to the side of the path. To achieve this, slope the path slightly in one direction, or crown the path in the centre to enable run-off to both sides of the path.

PATH MATERIALS

The materials you choose for your path will depend on factors such as:

• the style of your home;

• the formality or informality of your garden setting;

• your budget;

• the availability of materials;

• safety (non-slip paving materials are essential for paths that are exposed to the elements or located in areas prone to dampness or moss growth).

PAVING BRICKS AND BLOCKS

Bricks, pavers and blocks are popular materials for paving. Bricks and pavers are generally made from clay, while blocks are moulded from concrete. All are available in a wide range of colours, finishes and sizes.

Normal house bricks can be used for laying a path, provided they are frost proof, do not have perforating holes and are laid frog down if they have a recess (frog) on one side. Second-hand bricks can be obtained from demolition merchants and architectural salvage yards to match the paving to the house style.

Bricks are made to a 'module' size of 225 x 112.5 x 75 mm, where the length is twice the width and three times the thickness. Note that this module includes a 10 mm mortar allowance, so that the actual brick size is 215 x 102.5 x 65 mm.

Concrete blocks are generally made in smaller sizes, where the actual length of the block is twice its width and four times its thickness (for example, 200 x 100 x 50 mm). Clay pavers may be the same width and length as bricks or blocks but are usually 50 mm thick.

Bricks, blocks and pavers in which the length is twice the width can be used in more complicated patterns, such as herringbone or basketweave. Some concrete blocks are sold in interlocking geometric patterns, which are easy to lay.

PAVING SLABS

Paving slabs (flagstones) are generally made of concrete, with a smooth or textured finish, and are larger in width and length than bricks or blocks but less thick. A typical paving slab is 450 mm square and 40 mm thick, but other sizes are available.

Natural materials, such as stone or slate, cut into regular shapes, can also be used for paving and can provide an extremely attractive finish. The materials, however, are very expensive and not easy to lay because of the variation in size. Pieces of stone (especially Yorkstone) can be set on their own, or in conjunction with broken concrete paving slabs, to create 'crazy paving', laid on a bed of sand where the gaps between the stones are filled with mortar.

TILES

Tiles are available in a wide price range and vary from plain terracotta through to complicated tessellating patterns and colours. If choosing tiles, be sure that you have the necessary skills for laying them and choose a non-slip type for outdoor use.

STEPPING STONES

Stepping stones, whether of stone, concrete or timber, are a very practical and inexpensive option for narrow, low-use paths. Their ease of construction makes them a popular choice, particularly in areas where you want to protect the lawn or to make movement through a wet area possible. The disadvantage with stepping stones is that they are spaced to suit one individual's foot stride and this does not always suit everyone.

LOOSE MATERIAL

The use of loose material makes path construction very quick and easy. Materials range from large cobbles and small pebbles of various colours to irregularly-shaped quarry gravels. Their main disadvantage is their instability underfoot. They are also unsuitable for slopes, as the materials can wash away with heavy rain.

TIMBER
Owing to the durability of treated timber there has been a resurgence in the use of timber in paths, ramps and steps. Timber on or near the ground is prone to rot and attack from insects, but chemically-treated timber is protected from attack and can be used in paths with confidence (see Choosing timber, page 48), though it needs regular maintenance, especially if stained or painted.

COMBINATIONS
Paths can be constructed using two or more materials. Combinations such as brick and timber, or stone and gravel, are good choices. For the best effect, the path should work with, or blend into, the garden.

WHEN TO USE A PROFESSIONAL

With enough time and motivation, it is possible to complete the projects outlined in this book without consulting a professional. However, if you feel in doubt, do not hesitate to seek help or advice for some specific parts of your project. Here are some common problems and what to do.

PREPARING THE SITE
Many projects do not even get started because the site seems unsuitable for the planned project. If preparation involves the removal or deposit of large amounts of soil, hire a mechanical digger, to save time and energy.

DIFFICULT PATH PATTERNS
If you choose to lay a complicated tessellating pattern with tiles, you might need to consult an expert. This type of path looks very good, but it does need a high degree of skill to acquire a good result and to avoid frustration.

LAYING CONCRETE
It is not easy to lay concrete, especially if ready-mixed, so you may prefer to employ a builder for a concrete path or the concrete foundations for other types of path. Some ready-mixed concrete suppliers provide laying as an additional service.

STEPS
Another area that may require professional assistance is the construction of formal steps from brick, tile or slate. This may depend on how many steps you want to build (more than three or four steps can be daunting), so weigh up your skills and the time that you have before seeking help.

Path basics

Whatever style of path you decide to build, the basic steps for constructing it are essentially the same. The key to success lies in careful planning and thorough preparation of the foundations.

BASIC TOOL KIT

- String line
- Measuring tape
- Spirit level
- Straight-edge
- Shovel
- Spade
- Rake
- Hammer
- Rubber mallet
- Hand saw
- Screed rails and screed board
- Steel float
- Wooden float
- Permanent black marking pen
- Club hammer
- Bolster
- Wheelbarrow
- Broom
- Hose and nozzle

INITIAL PREPARATION
1 Decide on the style of path and pattern, and select the materials (see Planning your path, pages 4–9).

ORDERING MATERIALS
2 The next step is to order the materials for the path.
- To calculate the area of pavers, stone or tiles (sold by the m^2) required, multiply the length of the path by its width. To this measurement, add at least 5 per cent to cover breakage and cutting errors.

For example, a 12 m x 1.2 m path = 14.4 m^2
5 per cent = 0.7 m^2
Total area = 15.1 m^2

To calculate how many 200 x 100 mm paving blocks you need, multiply the area (m^2) by 50.

Thus, 15.1 m^2 x 50 = 755 pavers.

- Bedding material, usually sand, can be ordered by the tonne (ton) or by the cubic metre. A rule of thumb is 1.5 tonnes (1½ tons) to 1 cubic metre of bedding sand.

The main bedding material is sharp (building) sand, which is also used for making concrete. It has fine angular pieces of material.

To calculate the amount of bedding sand you need, multiply the surface area (in square metres) by the depth of bedding sand.

For example, 20 m^2 (area) x 0.025 m (depth) = 0.5 m^3. Using our rule of thumb correlation, 0.5 m^3 x 1.5 = 0.75 tonnes (¾ ton).

Contact your local supplier about the types of bedding materials

This path is laid in a diagonal herringbone pattern, edged by a square header course of bricks. The feature of this path is the central area of circular paving, set off nicely by a lavender bush.

available and check your order. It is always a good idea to purchase a little extra in case the depth of bedding material varies.

• Other materials you may need in small quantities are soft (bricklaying) sand and cement (for making mortar) and fine sand (for brushing into gaps in the paving). For small amounts of mortar (for example, for securing edges), consider buying dry ready-mix to which you simply add water.

LAYING OUT THE PATH
3 Lay out a straight path by stretching a string line on both sides

from beginning to end. Lay out a curved path by laying a hose or rope on the ground and adjust it to achieve a natural curve. Walk along the hose to see if the 'walk' is comfortable.

4 Have a final look at the layout of the path. Trust your instincts here. If it does not look right, adjust it until you are happy. It is easier to adjust it now than when you are laying the path.

5 Consider the width of the path. The width will be determined by the space available, as well as the purpose. A path for one person may be only 0.9 m wide, but a path for two people, side by side, will need to be at least 1.2–1.5 m wide. If possible, it is a good idea to make the width of your path suit the selected pathway materials. If you are using bricks or tiles, this will avoid unnecessary cutting.

EXCAVATION AND BASE PREPARATION

6 Check the degree of slope (see page 7) and decide whether the path needs to be level, ramped or stepped.

7 Set string lines to the finished height of the path. If you are laying a curved path, attempt to stretch one string line straight through the centre of the path as your finished height guide. When setting string lines, consider the need for water run-off and drainage. Try to give your path cross-fall to either a garden or grass area, preferably away from the house.

8 Excavate (if necessary) down to the appropriate depth, removing all vegetation. The depth below the string line will be determined by the thickness of the paving, plus the final depth of the bedding sand.

9 Check that your base is solid. If you find soft spots, particularly in clay-based soils, caused by poor drainage or broken pipes, dig out the suspect spots and redirect drainage or repair any broken pipes before building the path. Another way to ensure the base is firm is to rake cement through the surface of the base material, compact it with a compacting plate, hose it with water and allow it to set. If your base is solid, you should have no sinkage problems in the future.

Paths that have only pedestrian traffic do not usually need a sub-base of concrete or compacted hardcore. These are only necessary for vehicular traffic areas.

Bedding sand for paving needs to be between 25 and 50 mm in depth. Spread the sand over the path and rake it until it is roughly level.

SCREEDING

10 Screeding is the technique of levelling the bedding sand before laying the pathway materials. This removes any dips and bumps in the sand, which would otherwise give the finished path an uneven surface.

A level finish can be achieved by using one of two simple methods: the raised rail or the bedded rail method (see the box opposite).

SCREEDING

Level the sand using either the raised rail method or the bedded rail method.

RAISED RAILS

1 Place timber edges or rails at the finished string line height and peg or nail them in position.

2 Select a straight piece of timber (usually 100 x 50 mm), long enough to cover the width of the area to be screeded. Cut a notch from each end, 8–10 mm less than the thickness of the paving material to be laid. This allows for later compaction of the sand down to the finished height.

3 Drag the screed board over the top of the rails so that the sand is dragged back by it. Ensure the bedding sand is packed firmly. To make screeding easier, use a steel float to help push back, or remove to one side, the build up of sand that occurs behind the screed rail.

BEDDED RAILS

1 This is probably the easier method as there is less preparation and fewer materials are required. Use screed rails made from timber, aluminium or PVC conduit, or water pipe, and bed the rails into the sand (for narrow paths, only one rail is necessary). Make sure that the rails are below the finished string height by the same thickness as that of the pavers, less 8–10 mm for later compaction. To check this, place one of your selected pavers on the screed rail and check its height against the height to the string line (see step 4, page 18).

2 Using a straight piece of timber or a spirit level as the screed board, steadily drag it along the rails, screeding off and packing the sand to create a firm, level laying surface.

3 Remove the rails and fill the holes with more sand before you begin laying the path.

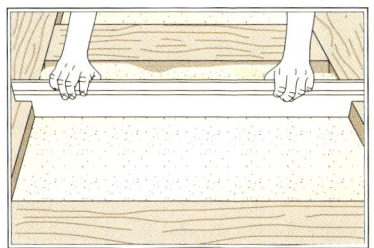

3 For the raised rail method, drag the screed board over the rails to level and pack the sand.

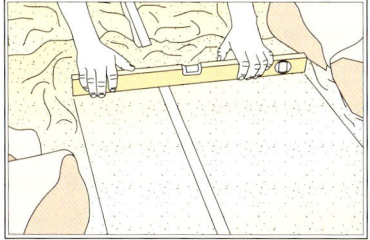

2 For narrow paths, use only one bedded screed rail and a spirit level to act as the screed board.

HINTS FOR SCREEDING

• Only screed off the sections of the path that you feel you can lay in your allocated time. After you have laid the bricks in the bulk of that section, re-set the rails and screed off the next section.

• Screeding is easier if the sand is kept moist.

LAYING THE PATH

11 Think about where you will start laying the path, as beginning in the right place will save you lots of paver or brick cutting later. For example, if the path travels along two walls of your home and meets at a corner, start laying at the corner first, and then lay away from the corner in both directions. This will avoid a cutting nightmare on the corner when the patterns of the two paths will not fit together.

Always lay the paving material against any solid structures, such as walls or fences, first and then lay in an outward direction towards an open space. This will avoid having to cut the last row of pavers.

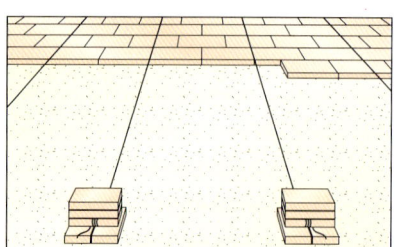

12 When laying a wide, straight path, set up three to four string lines. Lay the pavers following these lines.

12 Set up a guide to follow as you lay the path.

For straight paths, stretch a taut string line at the finished height of the path. Lay the paving materials to this line and the rest will follow. If the path is more than 1 m wide, a third or fourth string line is recommended to keep the path straight.

Curved paths are more difficult to lay. Use a hose or length of rope as your guide, and position it to create a free-flowing curve. Look at the curve from several different angles and adjust it until you are satisfied that you have no flat spots.

Circular paths are more difficult again and the ease of laying depends on your starting point. You can lay the path outside-in or inside-out.

• Outside-in. Place a peg in the centre of the site and insert a nail in the top of it to attach a string line. Stretch the string line taut while holding a stick and scribe a circle in the sand as a guide for laying. As you lay to the centre, you may need to cut whatever paving material you are using as the pattern becomes tighter. However, this will depend on the pattern selected.

• Inside-out. This is the more difficult of the two methods as you need to work in a confined space (the centre) with your material supply some distance away on the outside. One solution to this problem is to complete one half of the circle before beginning the other half, but make sure that your two halves match up exactly.

Crazy paving is a popular pathway material and looks wonderful in most settings. Here a stone path blends beautifully with this large country garden.

LAYING THE HEADER COURSE

13 A header course is a border or row of pavers running square or lengthwise to the path. The use of headers enhances a path as they:

• confine the paving within a border;

• provide strength for the edge of the path;

• set off the pattern enclosed;

• can be laid in a different colour to the main path to create a contrast;

• can be used as dividing strips to break larger areas into sections.

If possible, lay the first course of paving materials, or the header course, against your guide. Make any final adjustments to the header course before laying the rest of the path.

For further information see Edging styles, pages 58–61.

CUTTING PAVING MATERIALS

14 After the path has been laid with whole pavers or bricks, spaces will remain for filling in with cut pieces. Before cutting these materials, they have to be marked. Do this with a straight-edge and a permanent marker if you are cutting with a hired brick saw; any other drawn line will be washed away by the water running over the diamond-tipped saw blade.

15 Place the paver across the space left in the path so that it sits on the surrounding pavers. Scribe a line at the appropriate angle, approximately 5 mm in for a tight fit.

16 Cut the brick or paver using a bolster and club hammer, a block splitter, an angle grinder with masonry blade or a brick saw.

• If you use a bolster and club hammer, place the paver on a firm bed of sand. Tap around the four sides of the paver until it cracks. As you gain confidence, you will find that one short, solid blow will achieve the same result. Skutch hammers are useful for trimming the cut surfaces of pavers, brick and stone.

• Block splitters work best with concrete blocks. When used with bricks or clay pavers, the compressive action of the splitter tends to shatter bricks of baked clay.

• Angle grinders are effective but it is difficult to keep the cuts straight. This can be overcome by supporting the pavers within a framework. Cut tiles using an angle grinder with a masonry or diamond-tipped blade.

• Brick saws with diamond-tipped blades are the best for cutting pavers, bricks, stones or tiles. They are quick and provide a neat, straight cut. Brick saws can usually be hired on a short-term basis. Hand-operated tile cutters are also available for hire. To avoid excessive hire charges, have all your material marked ready for cutting prior to hiring.

17 Insert the cut paving materials into the spaces in the path.

COMPACTING

18 Compact the surface to bed the paving material in the sand. Pavers will sink about 5–8 mm when compacted, preventing future sinkage and creating a smooth, professional-looking surface. Check the line of pavers is straight and make any final adjustments.

Compaction can be done by hand or by machine.

• Compaction by hand. Use a rubber mallet to hit each paver individually to compact the path (this is very time consuming and it is difficult to compact each piece to the exact depth). Alternatively, use a club

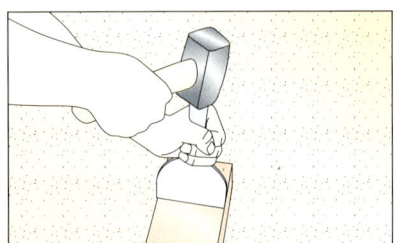

16 Place the paver on a firm surface and use a bolster and club hammer to cut it along the marked line.

18 Compact the pavers by hand using a straight-edge and club hammer. The straight-edge disperses the blow.

hammer and a straight-edge as wide as the path. Move the straight-edge slowly down the path, hammering along its top edge. This is a good way to compact cobbles and stones.

• Compaction by machine. For best results over a large area, hire a compacting plate. This is a petrol-driven machine with a motor that causes the bottom metal plate to vibrate up and down. As all pavers receive an even amount of pressure the surface is very level and neat.

19 Hold the edge of the pathway in place during compaction to prevent the pavers from moving. Use a piece of timber, or other type of straight-edge, to anchor the pavers (especially when using a compacting machine).

EDGING

20 There are many edging styles, but for the purposes of basic preparation this technique uses a 45 degree buttress of mortar against edging pavers (see Edging styles, page 58). This method is also suitable for edging stonework. Use a strong mortar (1 part cement to 3 parts sand).

Mix up sufficient mortar and cut the bedding sand away from the edge of the pavers with a spade or float.

21 Cut down to a solid base and shovel mortar along the edge of the border pavers. Use a float to create a 45 degree angle. The mortar should cover at least half the thickness of the paver. Allow the mortar to set. When the mortar sets, it holds the paving

---

HINT

Regrout the path every one to two years, as weathering and erosion gradually denude the joints.

---

materials in place and contains the bedding sand, preventing any future sinkage problems.

GROUTING

22 Grouting fills the joints and gaps between the pavers, bricks or stones to complete the path. As a grout material use either fine-grained sand, sifted soil (if you want to encourage moss growth) or a mix of 6 parts fine sand to 1 part cement, which will restrict weed growth. For tiles, a manufactured grout mix is available.

23 If using a dry mix of sand and cement as your grout, combine it in a wheelbarrow or on a board. Pre-mixed sand/cement grout can be bought in bags from paving suppliers.

24 Throw the dry mix over the dry surface of the path. If you throw dry mix on wet pavers, the cement may stain. Use a broom to push the mix into the joints. Sweep away the excess.

25 Hose the path using a nozzle set on a very fine spray, so as not to move the mix out of the gaps. Work across the surface in a systematic manner, ensuring that no cement is left on the surface to cause staining. The water will moisten the grout in the joints, which will then set and seal the path.

Brick or block path

Bricks, clay pavers and concrete blocks are hard-wearing, non-skid and offer a large range of colours. This path uses clay pavers, and because they are thinner than bricks they are easier to cut and lay. As the width of these pavers is exactly half their length, they are perfect for laying more complicated patterns such as herringbone.

TOOLS

• Basic tool kit (see page 10)
• Brick saw or angle grinder for cutting pavers (optional)

MATERIALS

• Brick pavers (clay)★
• Coarse-grained bedding sand
• Mortar mix for edging
• Fine-grained sand
• Cement

★ The pavers used for this path are 200 x 100 x 50 mm in dimension.

METHOD

1 Make the initial preparations and lay out the path following Path basics, pages 10–12. This path is straight and five paver lengths wide.

2 Set two string lines on each side of the path to the finished height level. Excavate the area to a minimum of 75 mm below the string line (90 mm for bricks). A firm base prevents sinkage problems later, so check the base and compact it if necessary.

3 Spread the bedding sand (35 mm deep) over the path area and rake it until it is roughly level.

4 Screed the sand using the bedded rail method (see the box on page 13). Place two screed rails in the sand following the string lines. Bed the rails into the sand about 40 mm below the string lines. Check the rail height by placing a paver on the rail against the string line. The paver should be 8–10 mm higher than the string line to allow for later compaction and settling.

5 Remove the two bedded screed rails and fill the rail grooves with sand. Then carefully level the surface with a float.

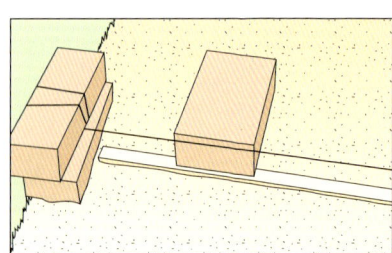

4 Bed the rails in the sand, and then check the height by placing the paver 8–10 mm higher than the string line.

Because brick pavers are geometrical in shape, they are best suited to a straight path. This path is laid in a 90 degree herringbone pattern, edged by a square header course of pavers.

6 Before laying the pavers, check for the best starting position. Lay both side header courses to the string lines, set to the path width.

7 Lay pavers in a herringbone pattern (see box on page 6) across the path to ensure they fit neatly within the string lines. If not, adjust the string lines and

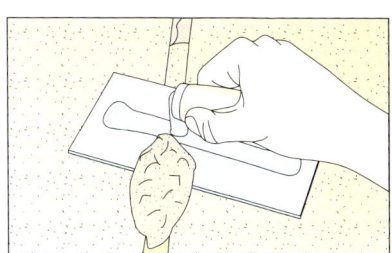

5 Remove the rails and fill the rail grooves with sand. Level the surface with a float.

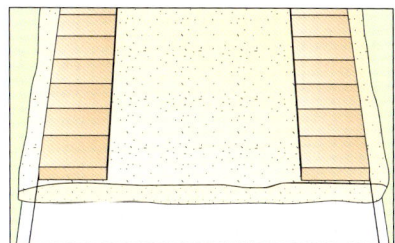

6 Lay both side header courses to the string lines. This will create an edge for the path.

This informal brick path blends beautifully with the rambling, overgrown garden it winds through. The bricks are second-hand house bricks and are laid using a combination of stretcher and stack bond patterns.

header courses accordingly. Do not lay the pavers too tightly, as they may vary slightly in length and width. A loose fit is best as this leaves enough room for adjustment and grout.

8 Once you have laid the whole pavers you will be left with spaces down each side for the half pavers.

Calculate how many halves you need, and then cut them all at once. A brick saw or angle grinder with a masonry blade is best for cutting clay bricks or pavers (see pages 15–16).

9 Place the half pavers into the spaces, with the cut edge facing towards the header course.

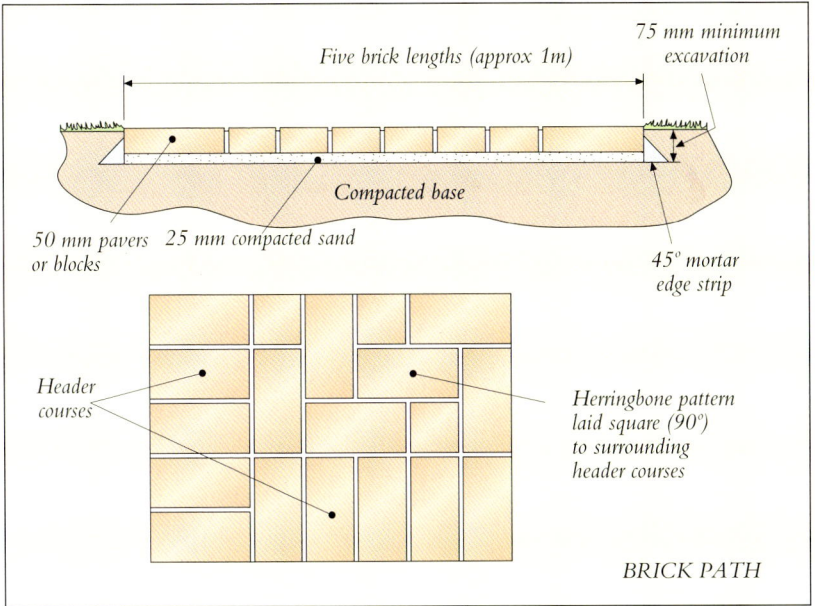

Five brick lengths (approx 1m)

75 mm minimum excavation

Compacted base

50 mm pavers or blocks

25 mm compacted sand

45° mortar edge strip

Header courses

Herringbone pattern laid square (90°) to surrounding header courses

BRICK PATH

10 With all the cut pavers in place, compact the path using one of the methods described on pages 16–17 of Path basics.

11 Edge the path (see pages 58–9). This path uses a 45 degree buttress of mortar against all unretained edges. The mortar edging must cover at least half the depth of the pavers.

12 To finish, grout the path. A dry mix of fine sand and cement is best in a ratio of 6:1 to help keep weeds at bay. Sweep the dry mix into all the joints, filling them thoroughly. (Keep any spare grout as the joints may need to be regrouted.) Hose the path with a fine water spray to clean the surface of the pavers and moisten the joints so that the grout will set hard.

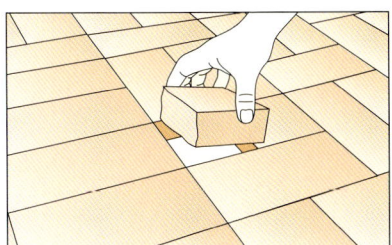

9 Cut the pavers in half and place them into the spaces, with the cut edge facing towards the header course.

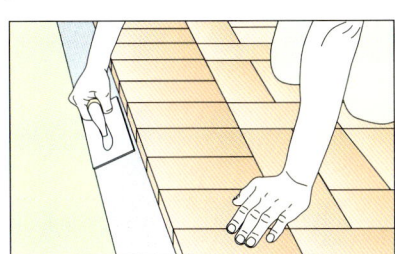

11 Edge the path with mortar. The mortar should cover half the depth of the pavers.

Crazy paving path

Crazy paving brings a warm, old-world charm to any setting and can be laid on almost any surface—soil, sand or concrete. Natural stone can vary in thickness, so you will often need to adjust the height of each piece in the bedding material as you lay it.

TOOLS

- Basic tool kit (see page 10)
- Angle grinder and masonry blade for cutting stone

MATERIALS

- Broken paving slabs and/or stones
- Coarse-grained bedding sand
- Mortar mix
- Fine-grained sand
- Cement

METHOD

1 Make the initial preparations and lay out the path (see Path basics, pages 10–12).

2 When excavating the area, extra depth may be required to allow for the varying thicknesses of natural stone. Spread a layer (50 mm deep) of coarse-grained sand over the path. The base should be firm to ensure the finished path is level.

3 Screed the sand using the bedded rail method (see pages 12–13).

4 Set up string lines if laying a straight path, or lay a piece of rope as a guiding edge for a curved path.

5 Group all the stones into piles of varying size and thicknesses. Lay the outer edges first using the largest stones, with the straightest edge against the guiding edge to neaten what is otherwise an informal jigsaw pattern of stone pieces. (As smaller stones tend to move, they are best laid

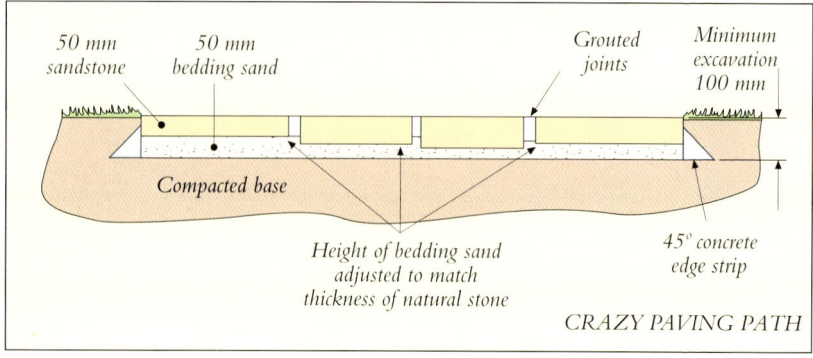

50 mm
sandstone

50 mm
bedding sand

Grouted
joints

Minimum
excavation
100 mm

Compacted base

Height of bedding sand
adjusted to match
thickness of natural stone

45° concrete
edge strip

CRAZY PAVING PATH

This crazy paving uses irregularly shaped pieces of stone fitted together like a jigsaw. For added strength, larger pieces of the stone are used on the outside of the path and smaller pieces towards the centre.

3 Using a straight piece of timber, screed off the excess sand to create a firm, level laying surface.

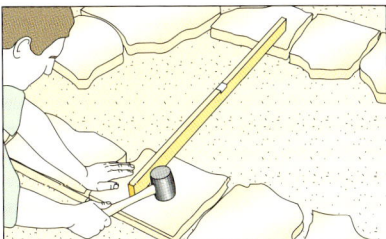

5 Lay the outer edges of the path first using the largest stones. Use a spirit level to check that the surface is level.

CUTTING STONE

If your stone is too thick to split with a hammer and bolster, cut halfway through from the underside of the stone with either a brick saw, or angle grinder and masonry blade. Complete the cut by driving wedges or the bolster into the cut, forcing the stone to split in a rough manner. This keeps the upper edges of the stone looking the same.

BUYING STONE

Natual stone is a heavy but very soft material, so it is easy for the home handyperson to cut and lay. It can be purchased new or second-hand. Artificial stone is also a popular pathway material as it is less expensive and much harder than real stone. It is sold in a variety of colours.

Stone can be purchased in either sawn or split forms. Sawn stone fits well in a formal setting as the regular geometrical pieces can be laid in a close, neat manner. Split stone, as used for this path, is irregular in shape and more suited to the creation of an informal atmosphere, with the stones being laid in a random manner.

When purchasing your stone, select pieces of similar thickness to make laying a level surface easier. Your stone should be at least 50 mm thick.

towards the centre.) Try to achieve a close fit, leaving a gap of 10–20 mm for grouting. If your stones are of different thicknesses, adjust the bedding sand by removing or adding sand to obtain a level, flat-topped surface. Check the surface using a spirit level. Tap the pieces in place with a rubber mallet.

6 Fill in any gaps with smaller pieces of stone. If you have to cut or trim the stone, use a hammer and bolster to maintain the split appearance of natural stone as a sawn edge will look out of place (see box on Cutting stone). To stabilise the smaller pieces, mortar them in place. Mix up a mortar using sand and cement in a 3:1 ratio, and add water to obtain a fairly firm, wet mix. Position the small stones on a bed of mortar.

7 Check the finished path is level, and then compact the stone by hand, using a rubber mallet, or a timber straight-edge and club hammer.

8 Edge and grout the path. This path is edged with mortar and uses a mix

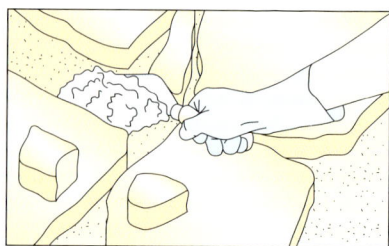

6 Fill in the gaps with smaller pieces of stone. Mortar them in position to ensure they remain stable.

of fine-grained sand and cement in a ratio of 6:1 for grouting (see Grouting, page 17). As grout shrinks slightly as it dries, you may need to regrout the path to fill the gaps.

MORTARING THE JOINTS

This path is grouted, but, if you want to have mortared joints, leave a wider gap of 15–20 mm between the stones. Mix a wet but stiff mortar and push it into the joints. Tidy up the excess with a small trowel. Use a paint brush and water to smooth the joints, and clean the face of the stone with a lightly-dampened sponge.

When laying a path using cut or sawn stone, keep the joints at 10 mm. Cut stone gives a more formal finish, so keep the joints consistent, similar to joints in a wall.

Fill the joint with a stiff mortar mix and sponge the surface clean. Once the joint has firmed again after sponging, use a pointing trowel to 'rake' the joint to give it an angular finish, or a rounded tool to give the joint a concave finish.

While crazy paving is often used in less formal settings, here we see it working just as nicely in quite a structured, formal garden. To finish the path, upturned pieces of stone are used to create a raised edging.

Concrete path

Concrete is a very adaptable construction material for paths as it can be formed into any shape desired. The wet concrete is held in place with formwork until it is dry. Once dry, concrete provides a solid walking surface that can be finished off in a variety of ways.

<table>
<tr><td>

TOOLS

- Basic tool kit (see page 10)
- Pliers
- Concrete mixer (if mixing your own)
- Gumboots
- Screed board
- Skip float
- Edging tool
- Jointing tool (home-made)
- Wooden float

</td><td>

MATERIALS

- Concrete★
- Timber formwork (see step 5)
- Timber pegs
- Nails
- Reinforcing mesh (optional)
- Tie wire
- 75 mm expansion material

★ If mixing your own concrete, see steps 1–2; if ordering ready-mixed concrete, see box on page 28.

</td></tr>
</table>

ORDERING CONCRETE

1 Concrete can be ordered ready mixed or be hand mixed on the job. If you want to mix the concrete yourself, be aware that there are different 'recipes' of concrete available for different jobs, whether for general purpose, foundations or paving. The recommended mix for paving consists of:

- 2½ parts coarse aggregate (gravel);
- 1½ parts fine aggregate (sand);
- 1 part cement;
- water to mix.

Rather than use separate sand and aggregate, you can buy 'combined aggregate', for which the mixture would be 1 part cement and 3½ parts 'combined aggregate'. You can also buy dry ready-mixed concrete (and mortar) to which you simply add water; this, however, is expensive for anything other than small jobs.

Small amounts of concrete can be mixed by hand on a large flat board. For quantities greater than 0.2 m³, you should consider hiring a concrete mixer, and for those greater than 0.5 m³ have concrete delivered ready mixed (see page 28 for details).

Dry cement is usually purchased in 50 kg bags from builders' merchants or DIY outlets. Store the bags in a dry place off the ground, on pallets if possible, as the cement will harden if left on the ground or on concrete floors. It is best, however,

Concrete is a practical and economical pathway material, useful for lengthy paths. This concrete path has been jointed at regular intervals to prevent cracking and has been finished with a wooden float to give it a non-slip surface.

to buy only as much as you need, as cement can take in moisture from the air and can harden.

CALCULATING CONCRETE QUANTITIES

2 Concrete quantities are worked out by the cubic metre (m^3). The area covered by a cubic metre is determined by the thickness of the slab. For example, if a slab is 100 mm thick, a cubic metre of concrete will cover 10 m^2. To calculate the amount of concrete you need, multiply length by width by depth. For example, a path that is 10 m long x 1 m wide x 100 mm deep would need 10 x 1 x 0.1 = 1 m^3 of concrete.

If your path requires a great deal of concrete (more than 0.5 m³) or if you do not want to mix your own, you can have it delivered by a lorry that is, in effect, a large concrete mixer on wheels.

When ordering ready-mixed concrete, check the minimum quantity the supplier will deliver (some have a minimum amount of 0.5 m³ or even 1 m³). Also make it clear what you want the concrete for, so that they can give you the correct mix.

The supplier will be able to tell you how long you have for barrowing the concrete from the lorry to the path (typically ½ hour per m³). You will certainly need to have everything ready, but check whether the supplier will provide his own wheelbarrows.

To order the materials required for a 1 m³ path (that is if you intend to hand mix your concrete), use the following quantities.

Concrete path (and all exposed paving)
• 8 bags cement
• 600 kg sand
• 1200 kg aggregate (or 1800 kg 'combined aggregate')

The corresponding figures (that is, per m³ of finished concrete) for the other two main types of concrete – general-purpose and foundation concrete – are as follows.

General purpose (most uses except foundations and exposed paving)
• 6½ bags cement
• 680 kg sand
• 1175 kg aggregate

Foundation concrete (foundations, footings, bases for pre-cast paving)
• 5½ bags cement
• 720 kg sand
• 1165 kg aggregate

PREPARATION
3 Make the initial preparations and lay out the path (see pages 10–12). This path is curved and 1.4 m wide.

4 Excavate and remove all vegetation to a depth of 100 mm below the finished height of the path.

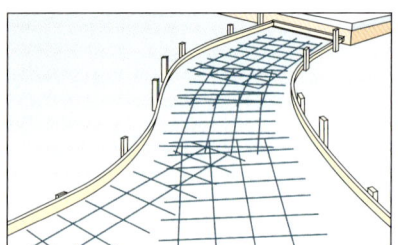

7 Place reinforcing mesh inside the formwork. Overlap the steel at least one and a half squares.

9 Spread out half the concrete; lift the steel mesh to the middle of the slab before adding the rest of the concrete.

5 Form up the timber edges to the predetermined levels. Give the path cross-fall to allow water to drain off. Peg and nail the formwork in position to create a strong edge, able to withstand the pressure of wet concrete. For straight edges, use either 100 x 50 mm or 75 x 50 mm timber. This curved path uses 100 x 10 mm timber offcuts, which are quite strong yet provide sufficient flexibility to shape the desired curve. The curves should be gradual, as tight curves are difficult to edge neatly.

6 If the area within the formwork needs filling, use sand which can be screeded off to the appropriate level (see Screeding, pages 12–13). If preferred, place plastic sheeting under the concrete to prevent rising moisture, although this is not necessary under a path.

7 For added strength, place reinforcing mesh inside the formwork. (Concrete paths can be constructed without using steel mesh, but it will avoid the path cracking at a later date, particularly if the slab

thickness is only 75 mm.) Overlap the steel mesh at least one and a half squares and set it 50 mm in from the formwork edging. Tie the steel mesh together with tie wire, using pliers.

8 If the concrete is to be laid against brickwork or other solid structures, it is advisable to place an expansion material such as hardboard between the wall and the proposed area of concrete. To fix the expansion material firmly against the brickwork, nail through it and into a brick joint. Set the joint at the finished concrete height. Add expansion joints on non-reinforced, long paths (see page 30).

LAYING THE CONCRETE

9 If you have ordered ready-mixed concrete, ensure that a wheelbarrow track is available and clear of obstacles for ease of delivery. Barrow the mixed concrete into position, and then spread and compact it using a square-nosed shovel. Once half your required depth is reached, lift the steel mesh to the middle of the slab before adding more concrete to top up to the finished height. If required, add expansion joints on long paths (see page 30). Pack the concrete tightly into all edges and corners of the formwork.

10 Screed off the excess concrete using a timber or aluminium straight-edge. Move the screed board slowly back and forth in a sawing motion to level off the concrete with the top of the formwork.

10 Move the timber straight-edge back and forth in a sawing motion to level off the excess concrete.

EXPANSION JOINTS FOR LONG PATHS

Where a path is longer than 2 m, you will need an expansion joint to prevent the concrete cracking. Such a joint absorbs the movement of the material and should run at right angles to the path.

The simplest way of creating an expansion joint is to insert a strip of expansion material (hardboard), propping it vertically with mortar while you fill the area on either side with concrete. If reinforcing mesh is used you will only be able to use a half-thickness joint.

For very long paths, you should also add dummy joints between the main expansion joints. These will ensure that if the concrete does crack it will do so in a single place without ruining the appearance of the concrete.

To form a dummy joint, press a T-shaped metal section into the concrete, or make a special tool with a thin protruding blade, which you can draw along a timber straight-edge.

11 Move a skip float (or a long, narrow float) lightly over the area to push the aggregate down, and to smooth and 'cream up' the surface ready for trowelling. This technique brings the wet mix of sand and cement to the surface and pushes the aggregate deeper into the concrete.

12 Use a hammer or mallet and tap along the side edge of the formwork. This helps to settle the edge concrete and prevents honeycombing. It will also prevent the edge from dropping when the concrete is later edged.

13 Use a hand-held float to 'cream up' the edges and to pack them hard prior to edging.

14 Roughly edge the path with a 75 mm L-shaped edging tool to push the stones down. If this is not done before the concrete hardens, it will be difficult to achieve a neat edge.

ADDING DUMMY JOINTS

15 To make a dummy joint (see box on left), calculate the position of the joints and mark them on the

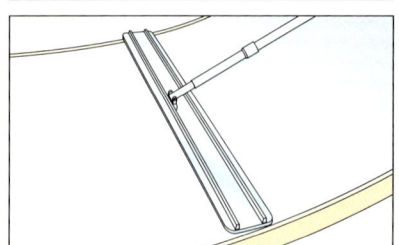

11 Move a large float over the surface to push the aggregate down and to smooth and 'cream up' the surface.

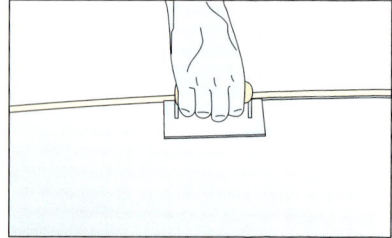

14 Roughly edge the finished path with a 75 mm edging tool to push the stones down.

formwork before pressing a T-shaped metal bar into the wet concrete. If using a jointing tool, place a straight-edge across the path on the marked position and hold the tool hard against the straight-edge.

FINISHING

16 Allow the concrete to dry to a point where only the surface is still workable. Generally this will take a few hours, depending on weather conditions. To finish the surface, use a wooden float and move it over the damp concrete in a circular motion to create a non-slip walking surface. (You can also use a broom, which will give you a grainier finish, or a steel float, for a smoother finish.)

17 Refinish the dummy joints and edging. The edging should be smooth with no breaks.

18 Allow the path to dry slowly. If concrete dries too quickly, cracks will appear in the surface. Keep the path moist for several days by covering it, or damping it with a hose to allow it to 'cure'.

Concrete can also be purchased ready made as square pavers, and laid in neat rows to make a wide path.

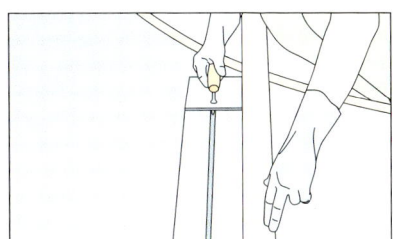

15 Hold a jointing tool hard against the straight-edge and cut a joint across the width of the path.

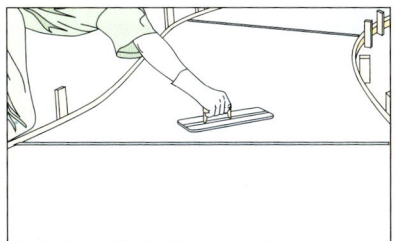

16 To create a non-slip surface, use a wooden float and move it over the damp concrete in a circular motion.

Tiled path

The rectangular or square geometry of a tiled path gives a formal look to the home. These paths differ from brick or crazy paving ones in that the tiles are laid on a concrete base, which needs to be in place well before tiling can commence.

TOOLS

- Basic tool kit (see page 10)
- Bolt cutters or angle grinder
- 10 mm notched trowel
- Pliers
- Tile cutter or brick saw
- Rubber squeegee
- Rubber gloves
- Firm sponges

MATERIALS

- 100 x 50 mm timber formwork
- Nails
- Steel mesh and ties
- Ready-mixed concrete
- Terracotta or other tiles★
- Acid for etching (optional)
- Tile adhesive and grout (see step 16)

★ This path uses 300 mm square tiles and is approximately 1.2 m wide.

CONCRETING THE BASE

1 Make the initial preparations and lay out the path (see pages 10–12).

2 Excavate the proposed area to a depth of 115 mm below the finished string line height (to allow for 100 mm of concrete, 5 mm of adhesive and 10 mm for the tiles.)

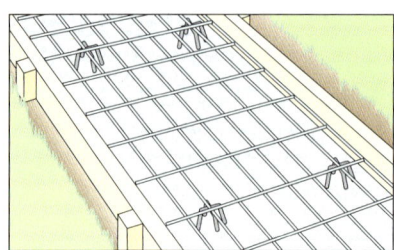

4 Place the mesh inside the formwork. Raise it in the centre of the slab using stirrups or other suitable material.

3 Form up the path; fix in place by nailing to pegs. (The internal spacing of the timber formwork for this path is 1.3 m.) Set the top of the formwork 15 mm below the finished string line height. This allows for the thickness of the tile and adhesive. (If you want cross-fall on the path, put cross-fall on the concrete formwork.)

4 Cut the mesh 1.2 m wide, using bolt cutters or an angle grinder. Place the mesh inside the formwork, 50 mm away from the inside edges, and overlap it at least two squares. Tie the mesh together using tie wire and pliers. Raise the mesh in the centre of the proposed slab, using

Terracotta tiles are very strong and durable. This path uses a stack bond pattern laid on the diagonal between longitudinal header courses.

supports. Alternatively, pour half the concrete and then lift the mesh up in the centre of the slab (see page 29).

5 Calculate the amount of concrete required by multiplying the length of the path by its width and depth.

For example, 20 m x 1.2 m x 0.1 m = 2.4 m³. See page 28 for how to estimate materials required and how to order ready-mixed concrete.

6 Pour the concrete on to the base and screed it off level with the top of the boards. To ensure better bonding with the tile adhesive, roughen the texture slightly with a wooden float.

LAYING THE TILES
7 While the concrete is curing (see box on page 34), plan the layout of the tiles. Do this carefully, particularly if you want a repeating pattern.

8 Dry lay at least 1 m of tiles out on the ground. If possible, cut the half and quarter tiles to complete the pattern and lay them in position.

CURING CONCRETE

New concrete requires curing time. It is often recommended that one month be allowed for curing for each 25 mm thickness of slab before tiling with a cement-based adhesive.

Adjust the pattern, allowing a 10 mm gap for grouting, and check that it will fit properly on the path. Set string lines for the outer edge of the border courses to the final width.

9 Place the tiles on the concrete and trace around them with a permanent black marker. This will make it easier to follow the pattern once you start laying the tiles.

10 To ensure maximum adhesion of the tiles, mix the acid and water in a 1:10 ratio (add acid to the water to prevent the acid from splashing up and burning you). Spread it over the concrete and rub it in with a stiff-bristled broom. Rinse the surface with water and allow the concrete to dry.

11 If the pattern is repetitive, pre-cut the tiles, or cut them after laying the whole tiles (see step 16, page 16).

12 Cut the half tiles for the header courses, and lay them on both sides of the path to the string lines. Mix enough tile adhesive to lay about 1 m² of tiles at a time (ask your tile supplier for the correct adhesive). Spread the adhesive with a notched trowel.

13 Press each tile firmly on to the adhesive and tap with a rubber mallet to remove any air bubbles.

14 Check the height between the header courses (or edges) with a spirit level and straight-edge.

15 Lay the centre of the path using full and diagonal half and quarter tiles. Lay the tiles using the two header courses as your guide for spacing and height. Check the diagonal lines are straight and the surface is even.

16 Allow the tiles to set and grout the joints. Purchase pre-mixed grout from your tile supplier, or mix your own using fine-grained sand and cement in a 4:1 ratio. Mix the grout with water to obtain a firm consistency. Work on an area of 1 m² at a time.

17 Use a rubber squeegee or sponge to work the mixture into the joints.

18 Remove the extra grout from the tile face with a soft, clean sponge and minimum water. Give the tiles a final clean down after the grout has set.

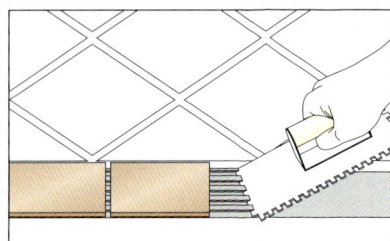

12 Spread the adhesive with a notched trowel, and lay the header course of tiles on both sides of the path.

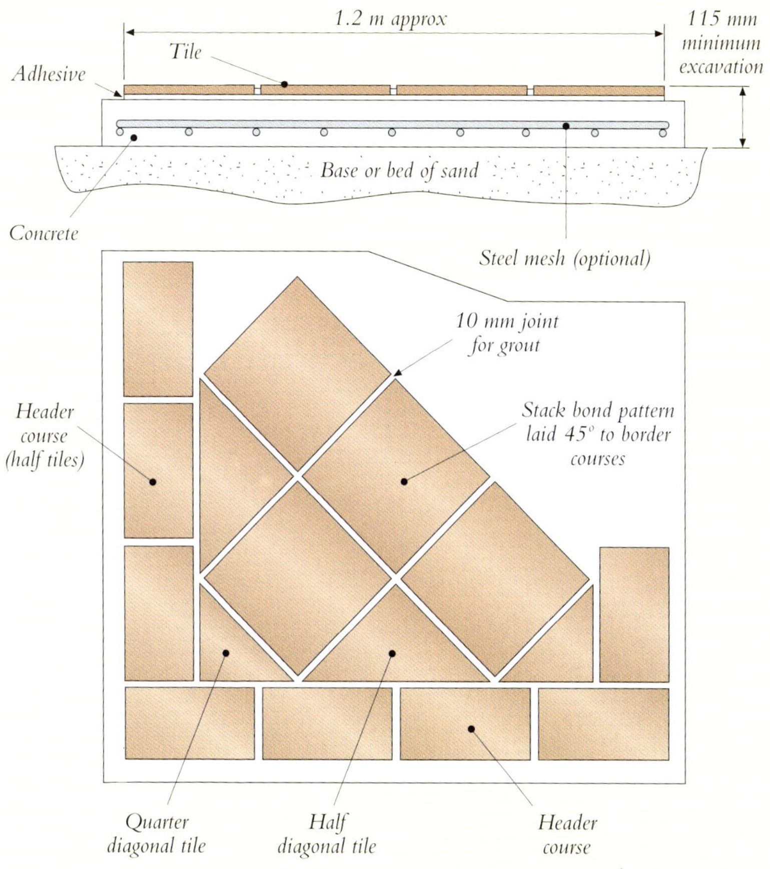

1.2 m approx

115 mm minimum excavation

Tile

Adhesive

Base or bed of sand

Concrete

Steel mesh (optional)

10 mm joint for grout

Header course (half tiles)

Stack bond pattern laid 45° to border courses

Quarter diagonal tile

Half diagonal tile

Header course

TERRACOTTA TILED PATH

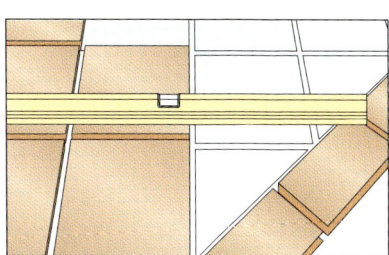

15 Lay the centre of the path. Use a spirit level to make sure that the finished surface is even.

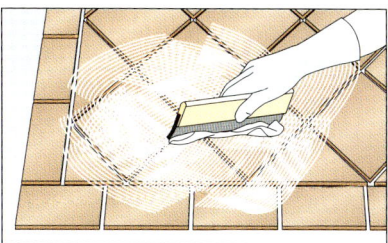

17 Using a rubber squeegee, work the grout thoroughly into all the joints. Wear gloves to protect your hands.

Stepping stone path

The use of stepping stones creates an informal and easy-to-construct path, which can be laid in straight or curved lines with equal ease. A stepping stone path is ideal for areas that are constantly moist or wet underfoot, or areas such as lawn that begin to show signs of wear from foot traffic.

TOOLS

- Basic tool kit (see page 10)
- Chain saw (if cutting your own timber rounds)

MATERIALS

- Stepping stones (timber rounds)
- Coarse-grained bedding sand

METHOD

1 To lay timber rounds across a grassed area, step out the area where the path will be, marking each stride as the location for each round. Lay the rounds on the grass and walk across them to check the stride spacing. If necessary, adjust the distance between the rounds. Do not have them too far apart as this will make walking uncomfortable. If someone else is going to be using the path, it is a good idea to ask them to check the stride spacing for comfort also. As a general rule, the average adult stride is between 600 mm and 700 mm when measured from centre to centre.

2 With the timber rounds in place, examine the line taken by the path and adjust it until you are happy with the direction and shape.

3 Leave the rounds in place and cut around them with a spade or lawn edger. Remove each round and set it aside. Dig out sufficient soil to allow for the depth of the timber round,

1 Lay the timber rounds on the grass, and then check the stride spacing, adjusting the rounds if necessary.

3 Leaving the timber rounds in place, use a spade or lawn edger to cut out the grass around them.

Stepping stones are suited for light traffic areas, such as a path leading to the clothes line or garden shed, and are less intrusive across a lawn than a path. The stones are set level with the ground to make lawn mowing easier.

plus approximately 50 mm of coarse-grained bedding sand.

4 Add the bedding sand and level the surface roughly with a float or trowel. Tamp the surface to ensure it is well compacted. Coarse-grained sand is a better bedding sand than some of the fine-grained sands, because it compacts to a firm base

4 Add 50 mm of coarse-grained sand and level the surface roughly with a float or trowel.

Concrete paving slabs are a good option for a stepping stone path. Here the thick plantings of grass give the path a less formal appearance, as the plants spill on to the pathway, softening the edges.

SELECTING STEPPING STONES

Stepping stones can be made from a variety of materials, all of which are laid on a sand bed.

• Precast concrete slabs are available in a variety of shapes and colours, and are well suited to a formal garden setting. Round, square, rectangular and kidney shapes are common and come in a range of sizes to suit the situation.

• Timber rounds look well in a natural setting. They are cut from a variety of hardwoods to a minimum thickness of about 50 mm. Softwood timber is not recommended, because direct ground contact will lead to rot, insect and fungal attack. To increase the life of the timber, coat the rounds with preservative before laying them. Preservative-treated rounds can be purchased ready-cut. If you are able to obtain suitably-sized timber, cut your own stepping stones using a chain saw.

• A flagstone is any flat, irregularly shaped stone or rock. Although heavy and sometimes difficult to find, the natural colours and durability of this type of stone make it an excellent choice as a path material. When selecting stones, choose large pieces of similar thickness.

• For a more formal approach, create stepping stone pads from bricks laid at intervals. Usually two, three or four bricks are sufficient for each pad.

and, at the same time, provides good drainage qualities.

5 Place the round in position and tap the surface with a rubber mallet. Check the surface is level using a spirit level. Continue in this manner until all the rounds are in position.

6 To complete the path, fill in around the edges of the rounds with clean soil plus grass seed.

5 Place the timber round in position and tap the surface using a rubber mallet to settle it in place.

HINTS

• When laying in a lawn, make sure that the rounds or stones are settled at ground level for ease of mowing.

• If laying rounds or stones in a loose material path, raise them slightly so the gravel or bark does not scatter over them.

Cobbled path

Cobbles are large, round stones or shingles that are found on beaches and in rivers. Cobbled paths can be straight or curved, since the loose material needs only to be stabilised and contained within formwork.

TOOLS

• Basic tool kit (see page 10)

MATERIALS

• 100 x 38 mm preservative-treated pine (rails)
• 100 x 38 mm preservative-treated pine (pegs)
• Fifty 50 mm (2 in) twisted, flat-head, galvanised nails
• Fine-grained sand
• Cement
• Cobbles

METHOD

1 Make the initial preparations and lay out the path following the instructions for Path basics, pages 10–12. Set the string lines to the

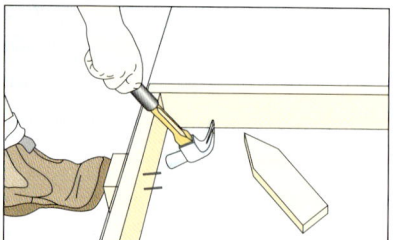

4 Fix pegs on the outside of the rails, spacing them 1.2 m apart. The pegs will support the timber edges.

finished height and spacing for the path. This path is 1.2 m wide.

2 Excavate and remove all vegetation to a depth of 100 mm below the finished height of the path.

3 Using 100 x 38 mm treated pine, form up the rails to be used as timber edges for the cobble path (see the box on Choosing timber, page 48). Set the timber edges to the finished string line height.

4 Cut the 100 x 38 mm pointed pegs and hammer them into the ground on the outside of the rails every 1.2 m. Fix the timber pegs to the nails using 50 mm (2 in) nails. The pegs should be approximately 300–450 mm long, depending on the soil type. The finished height of the peg is approximately two-thirds of the finished height of the rail.

5 Re-seal any cut surfaces on the rail or pegs with preservative to ensure protection from ground contact.

6 This path is screeded using the raised rail method (see the box on screeding, page 13). Cut a notched

Cobbles have excellent drainage and drying qualities, and they provide a wonderful contrast and colour emphasis within the garden. Gardens with an oriental influence often feature cobbled paths in their formal designs.

screed board from a piece of timber that is wider than the path. Cut notches in both ends so that the screed board sits inside the edging rails to a depth of 50 mm.

7 Mix up a dry mortar mix of fine-grained sand and cement in a ratio of 3:1. Spread the dry mortar mix between the rails, 50 mm deep.

HINT

Cobbled paths have a rustic appearance, but they can have a very uneven surface which can be uncomfortable to walk on. To make the path easier to walk along, consider placing stepping stones along the middle of the path, within the cobbles.

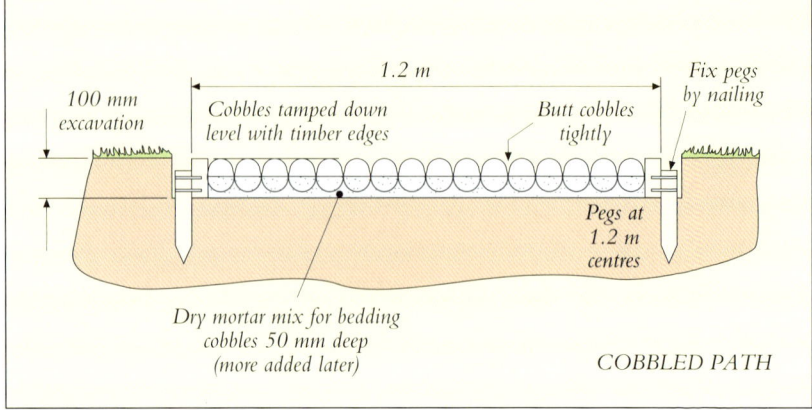

100 mm excavation

1.2 m

Cobbles tamped down level with timber edges

Butt cobbles tightly

Fix pegs by nailing

Pegs at 1.2 m centres

Dry mortar mix for bedding cobbles 50 mm deep (more added later)

COBBLED PATH

8 Pull the screed board over the rails to level the surface.

9 Position the cobbles tightly together on the surface of the dry mortar mix.

10 Use a timber straight-edge and a club hammer to tap the cobbles and press them firmly and evenly into the dry mortar mix. The cobbles should be recessed into the mix to at least half their depth.

11 Add more dry mortar mix to the surface of the path so the level is as close to the finished height of the cobbles as possible. Remember, when you add water to the dry mix, the finished height will drop. Use a broom to sweep the mix into the spaces between the cobbles.

12 Set the hose nozzle on a fine spray and moisten the entire path with water. This will wash the cobbles clean and soak the dry mortar mix so that it will set firmly, holding the cobbles in place.

13 Allow the mortar to dry and, for a smoother finish, add an extra layer. Leave this to set.

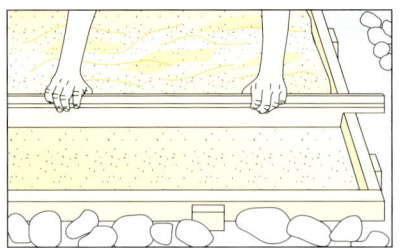

8 Using a notched screed board, pull it over the rails to level the surface of the dry mortar mix.

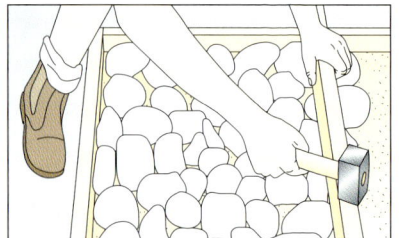

10 Using a timber straight-edge and a club hammer, tap the cobbles to press them firmly into the dry mix.

MAINTENANCE OF BRICK AND BLOCK PATHS

Regular maintenance will keep your path looking neat and tidy, and it will also eliminate the dangers associated with mossy growth. Here are some common problems and how to fix them.

• Efflorescence appears as a white powdery discoloration on the surface of new bricks or pavers. It is caused by soluble salts being brought to the surface by moisture.

To remove it, use a stiff-bristled brush or broom to brush it off until the powder ceases to form. Do not wash it with a hose as this only dissolves the crystals back into the brickwork to reappear again.

• Moulds, lichens and mosses love damp conditions. They are dangerous on paths as they make them very slippery and the paths need to be cleaned regularly.

To reduce the problem, check that moisture is not accumulating in the area due to broken or leaking pipes. If possible, expose the area to more sun by removing or pruning overhanging plants or trees. This will allow the path to dry out, lessening the likelihood of excessive moss growth.

When cleaning off the growth, remove the surface mould with a spade or stiff-bristled brush, and treat the area with a bleach or a fungicidal solution, following the manufacturer's instructions. The stains and discoloration left behind on the bricks or blocks are more difficult to remove, but they should fade over time if the area is exposed to more sun.

• Paths can also be cleaned by using an acid-based cleaner and high-pressure washer. If you adopt this method, work very carefully and wear protective clothing.

REMOVING BRICKS OR BLOCKS
If stubborn or unsightly stains on paths refuse to budge, turn the bricks or blocks over, presenting a new face to rejuvenate your path.

1 To remove tightly compacted bricks or blocks, wiggle two screwdrivers into the joints at either end. Prise the brick or block out carefully, working the two screwdrivers downwards.

2 Once one brick or block is out, the rest can be lifted by hand.

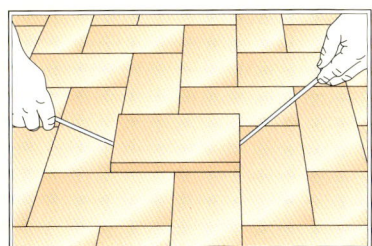

1 Push two screwdrivers down the sides of the brick or block and prise it out slowly.

Timber walkway

A timber walkway can be constructed on level land or be ramped or stepped to suit sloping sites, and its versatility means that it can be laid both on the ground or above it. For this walkway, the bearers rest on small posts, and metal brackets connect the joists to the bearers. The path slats are then nailed to the joists.

MATERIALS★

- 100 x 100 x 400 mm timber (posts)
- 100 x 100 x 1000 mm timber (bearers)
- 150 x 50 x 1500 mm timber (joists)
- 100 x 25 x 1200 mm timber (slats)

OTHER: Gravel or pebbles for drainage; brackets; 40 mm (1½ in), 50 mm (2 in), 75 mm (3 in) twisted, flat-head, galvanised nails; dry-mix concrete; polythene sheeting

★ This walkway is constructed using planed, preservative-treated softwood (see Choosing timber, page 48)

TOOLS

- Basic tool kit (see page 10)
- Hand saw or circular saw
- Sander

METHOD

1 Before constructing the path, fill areas of high water retention with gravel or pebble to improve drainage.

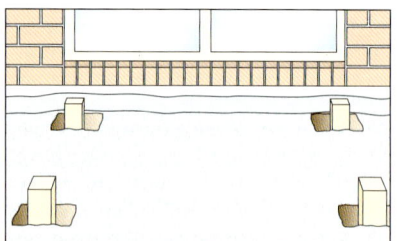

5 Place posts in the holes at 900 mm centres, ensuring they are 115 mm below the finished height of the path.

Make the initial preparations and lay out the path following the steps in Path basics, pages 10–12.

2 Lay out the path using two string lines, one string line for each row of posts. Set the string lines exactly 900 mm apart and at the finished height of the path.

3 Drive stakes into the ground to mark the positions of the posts at 1.5 m spacings along the path.

4 Excavate the holes for the posts to a minimum depth of 300 mm. Hole depth is governed by the height of the timber path and the soil type.

5 Place posts in the holes at 900 mm centres across the path. Make sure that the posts are 115 mm below the finished height of the path. (If the posts extend beyond the finished post

height, identify the cut-off line with a string line and spirit level. Mark and cut off square with either a hand or circular saw.) Use a spirit level to check that the posts are vertical, and then concrete them in position. Slope the concrete slightly to encourage the water to run away from the posts. Leave the concrete to set for two to three days.

An alternative to setting the posts in concrete is to set them in metal brackets above the ground, as can be done with fence or pergola posts.

6 Spread the polythene sheet beneath the path area to reduce weed growth and cover it with approximately 50 mm of pebbles or gravel to improve drainage.

This timber walkway runs along one side of the house. To finish the walkway off neatly, a brick wall has been built on its outer edge, using the same type of mortar joint as those on the house.

7 Decide which way the decking is going to run as the bearers will run in the same direction. In this case, the slats run across the walkway, so the bearers are positioned across the top of the posts. Skew-nail the bearers to the top of the posts using 75 mm (3 in) twisted, flat-head nails, or alternatively fix them in position with gang nail plates.

8 Position the joists at right angles to the bearers to keep the walkway close to the ground. The joist tops should sit flush with the bearer tops. Cut three joists to 1.5 m lengths, position them between the bearers and fix with metal brackets or joist hangers. The metal brackets are fixed to the inside of the bearers and posts with 40 mm (1½ in) flat-head nails.

Place the joists at 450 mm centres, one joist on each outside edge and one in the middle. (The joists are positioned flush with the top of the bearers to keep the path at a height of approximately 200 mm, but if you have room to raise the walkway, fix the joists to the top of the bearers.)

ALTERNATIVE

If your path is against the side of the house, one bearer can be screwed directly to the wall, removing the need for posts beneath that bearer. The decking slats should then run parallel to the wall, because the joists would be at right angles to the wall.

SAFETY

When working with preservative-treated timber, you should wear a protective dust mask and gloves while sawing and planing. Do not burn these products as the smoke and ash can be toxic. Dispose of any offcuts by burying them.

ADDING THE SLATS

9 Lay the decking slats at right angles to the joists. Fix the first slat, making sure that it is square, giving it a 100 mm overhang on one side. Do the same with the last decking slat, but do not drive the nails in completely as this last slat will

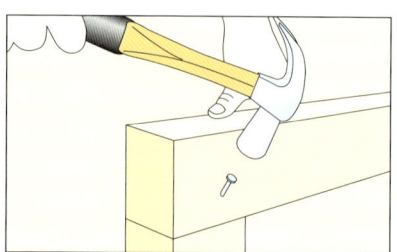

7 *Position bearers across the top of the posts, running in the same direction as the decking. Skew-nail into position.*

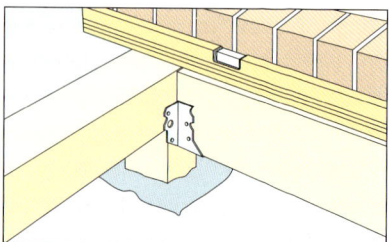

8 *Using metal brackets, fix the joists to the bearers. Place one joist on each outside edge and one in the middle.*

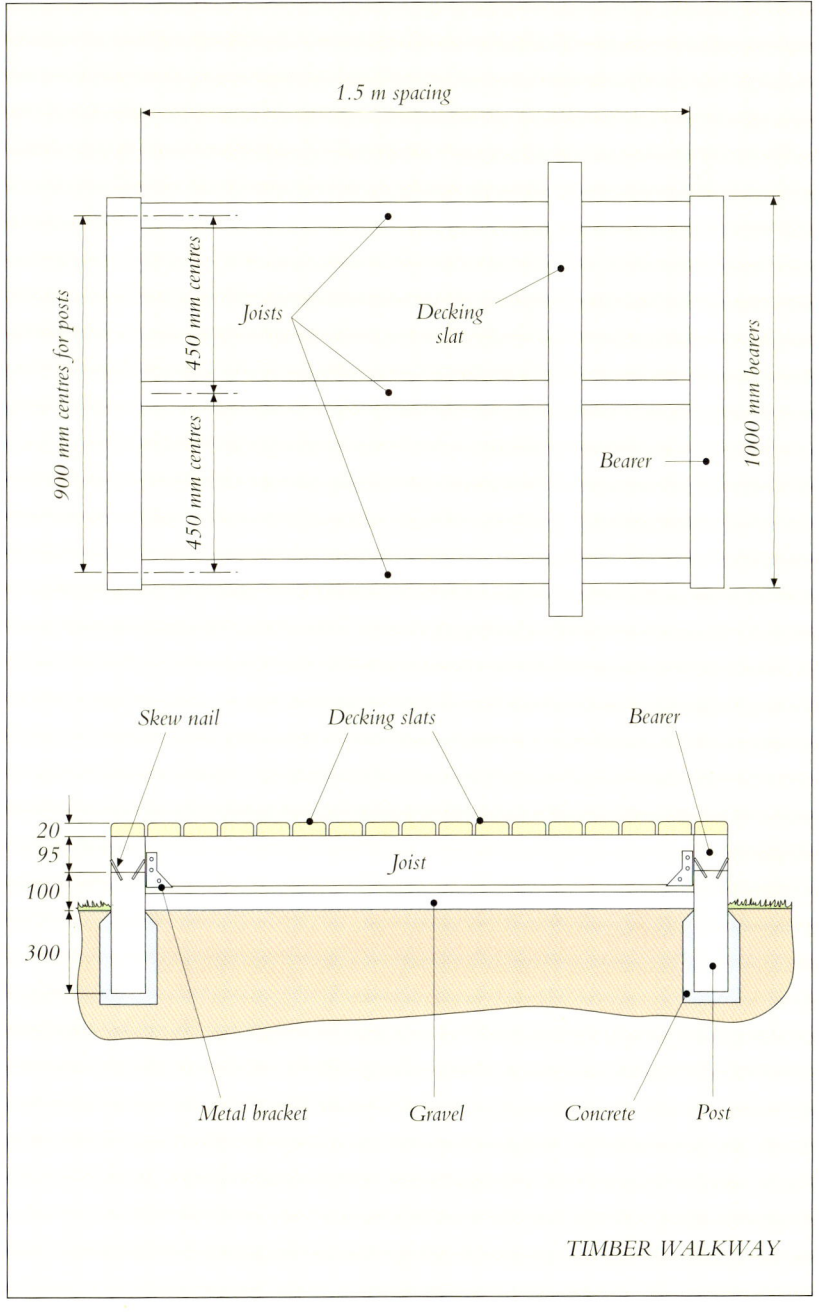

1.5 m spacing

900 mm centres for posts

450 mm centres

450 mm centres

Joists

Decking slat

Bearer

1000 mm bearers

Skew nail

Decking slats

Bearer

20
95
100
300

Joist

Metal bracket

Gravel

Concrete

Post

TIMBER WALKWAY

CHOOSING TIMBER

Timber paths can be constructed from hardwood or preservative-treated pine. During their life span, timber paths have to withstand the ravages of weather and attack by insects and fungi, so discuss the options with your local timber merchant.

Preservative-treated timbers are softwoods that have been made resistant to attack and rot through chemical processing. These timbers are easier to work with than hardwood, making them more attractive for use by the home handyperson.

Even though many hardwoods are more resistant to attack, any that come into contact with the ground will also need to be treated with a preservative such as creosote. Any cut or planed section of timber should be re-sealed or re-treated before coming into contact with the ground. Products for re-sealing are available from your timber merchant.

POST MATERIALS

As these are in contact with the ground they are constantly being subjected to attack by moisture, fungus and insects. Choose either one of the most durable hardwoods or a pressure-impregnated softwood from your local timber merchant.

BEARERS AND JOISTS

Because these are not usually in contact with the ground, select from any durable hardwood or preservative-treated softwood, depending on your budget.

DECKING SLATS

These should not be in contact with the ground. Select from moderately durable hardwood or preservative-treated softwood.

Ensure you use galvanised nails and fasteners for timber used outside. Not only will plain steel nails rust, but they can also react with, and discolour, the timber.

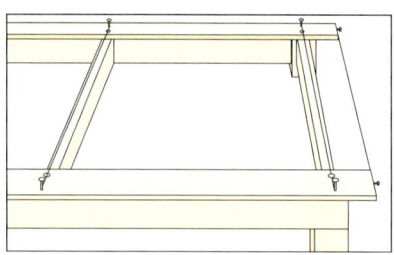

9 Fix the first slat and temporarily tack the last slat in place. Run a string line between the two slats.

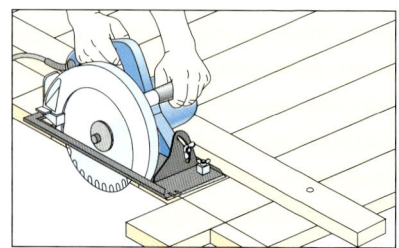

10 Trim the overhang using a circular saw. Tack a timber straight-edge along the slats as a guide for the saw.

A timber walkway can be incorporated into a pathway to bypass areas that have poor drainage. Use durable hardwood or preservative-treated softwood to reduce the chance of the wood deteriorating, due to constant exposure to damp.

probably need repositioning. Run a taut string line from the outside edge of the two 100 mm overhangs. This is your positioning guide for each slat before it is fixed with 50 mm (2 in) flat-head nails. (It also helps to set string lines as a guide for your nails to follow.) Lay the slats across the joists, fixing them with two nails per slat at each joist position.

10 The opposite side of the decking may have an uneven overhang. To trim up the edges, run a taut string line from the first to the last decking slat, providing for a similar 100 mm overhang. Mark the slats with a pencil and trim off with a hand or circular saw. Tack a timber straight-edge along the slats as a guide for a circular saw.

11 Finish by sanding any rough edges to remove splinters. Paint or stain the timber, or leave it natural.

WHY TIMBER PATHS?

Because timber paths are usually slightly elevated above ground level, they are invaluable in overcoming problems such as steep slopes or poor drainage. Steep sites generally require filling, levelling and then retaining before a normal path can be laid, but timber paths can be used as bridges or ramps.

Loose materials

Paths can be constructed from a variety of loose materials, ranging from stone and gravel, to wood or bark chip, leaf mulch, or coarse and fine-grained sands. The materials are contained by lengths of treated softwood.

TOOLS

- Basic tool kit (see page 10)
- Spade

MATERIALS

- 75 x 50 mm preservative-treated softwood (rails)
- 75 x 50 mm preservative-treated softwood (pegs)
- 75 mm (3 in) twisted, flat-head, galvanised nails
- Polythene sheeting (optional)
- Loose material

METHOD

1 Make the initial preparations and lay out the path (see Path basics, pages 10–12).

2 Set string lines at the finished height and spacing for the path. This path is 900 mm wide.

3 Remove all vegetation and excavate the proposed area to a depth of approximately 50 mm below the finished height of the path. Crown the base of the path, or provide cross-fall from one edging rail to the other to assist any water to drain away from the path.

4 Using a spade, dig a 20 mm deep trench along the string lines so that the pine edging will fit flush with the string line. Digging the edge rail into the base ensures that the loose material will not wash away from under the edge during heavy rain.

5 Form up edge rails to confine the path (see Cobbled path, page 40), using 75 x 50 mm timber, and fix with the pegs. Re-seal any cut surfaces to prevent the timber rotting when in contact with the ground (see Choosing timber, page 48). Alternative edges to confine loose materials are rock, sleepers, bricks, treated logs or concrete kerbs.

6 Lay the polythene sheeting down between the timber edge rails to discourage weed growth.

7 Spread the loose material over the sheet, 50 mm deep, to bring it level with the top of the edging rails. Do not have too much depth as this will create more movement, making it difficult to walk along the path.

LAYING STEPPING STONES IN LOOSE MATERIAL

1 Excavate the entire path area and form up the edges with preservative-treated pine timber. Peg and fix in place.

2 Place the stepping stones of your choice in position, checking the stride spacing. If the stones seem at risk of movement, anchor them in place with a bed of mortar.

3 Fill around the stepping stones and up to the timber edging with a loose material of similar origin, such as timber rounds surrounded by bark chip, or concrete stepping stones surrounded by gravel. (An alternative is to set the stones close together and use any of the loose materials as infill for the small spaces that are left.)

This path uses a rough, stone-like, loose material. The raised edging prevents the stones from scattering over the lawn.

Brick and timber path

Wonderful paths can be created by combining a variety of materials. They can be a combination based on texture, colour or size. This rustic path is constructed using old house bricks and railway sleepers.

TOOLS

- Basic tool kit (see page 10)
- Circular saw
- Electric drill and bits

MATERIALS

- Old railway sleepers
- 75 mm (3 in) lost-head, galvanised nails
- Coarse-grained bedding sand
- Bricks
- Fine-grained sand
- Cement

LAYING THE SLEEPERS

1 Make the initial preparations and lay out the path (see Path basics, pages 10–12).

2 Set the string lines to the finished height and with an internal spacing between parallel sleepers of four brick lengths. To avoid cutting bricks, lay out the pattern on the ground to make sure the spacing will fit your pattern.

3 Remove all vegetation and excavate the ground to the depth of the railway sleepers.

4 Place the railway-sleeper edgings in position, setting them lengthwise to the two string lines.

5 Using a circular saw, cut the remaining railway sleepers to fit across the path. Place these cross sleepers in position to create bays to take five brick widths. The sleepers

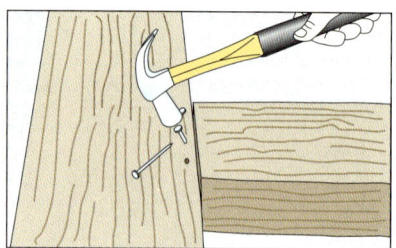

5 Place the cross sleepers in position to create the bays. Fix them together by skewing nails across the joint.

7 Pack the sand firmly in the bays and level off the excess using the screed board.

This combination of brick and railway sleepers looks well in an informal garden, but bear in mind that building such dual-material pathways requires more time spent in organisation and construction.

have butt or square joints, fixed together by skewing 75 mm (3 in) lost-head nails across the joint. Use three nails per joint to hold the sleeper framework together. Pre-drill the holes to prevent the wood from splitting. Using a spirit level, check the surface is level.

6 Prepare a notched screed board (see step 6 of the Cobbled path, page 40), making the notch 8–10 mm less than the brick thickness to allow for later compaction.

7 Fill the bays with sufficient coarse-grained bedding sand for screeding.

Brick and concrete are also good choices when it comes to planning a combination path. Here old bricks are laid around concrete slabs, and the path is edged by bricks placed on their side.

SELECTING MATERIALS

Combination paths provide a meeting place for various elements in the landscape, where aspects such as texture and colour can be contrasted or blended.

Before selecting your materials, decide whether you want harmony or contrast in the finished path. Harmonious combinations have similar colours and are of similar material origin, such as timber stepping stones and bark chip, or bricks and gravel. Contrasting combinations can be based on colour or choice of materials, such as a white pebbled path edged with red bricks, or brick paving with timber, used as a dividing header and edging.

When selecting materials for a combined path, limit your choice to only two or three to avoid a piecemeal appearance.

Pack the sand firmly and screed off the excess. This path is screeded using the raised rail method (see the box on page 13).

ADDING THE BRICKS

8 Lay the bricks in a stretcher pattern (if preferred, other patterns can be used). Lay the whole bricks first, and cut the half bricks. A club hammer and bolster will easily cut house bricks.

9 Firm the bricks down. A club hammer and timber straight-edge are sufficient for compacting the bricks for this path. The straight-edge should be long enough to cover the width of the path. Move the straight-edge down the path, hitting along the top of the wood with the hammer. As the bricks are held in place by the timber edging, there is no need to hold the edge bricks in place during this process.

10 Grout the bricks with fine sand or a dry mortar mix (of 6 parts sand to 1 part cement). Use a stiff-bristled broom to sweep the sand or mix into the joints. Sweep away the excess, and finish by hosing off with a fine spray of water (see page 17).

11 To build the single sleeper step, refer to the instructions on page 66.

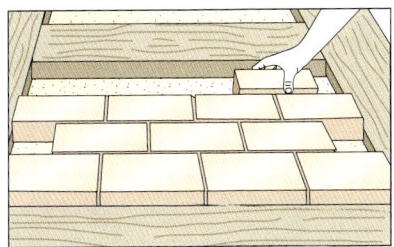

8 Lay the bricks in a stretcher pattern. Fill the bays with the whole bricks first.

9 To ensure the bricks are level with the timber, compact them using a club hammer and straight-edge.

Stone and gravel path

This type of path is suited to both an informal and formal setting. The path is bordered on one side by split pieces of natural stone and is filled with coloured gravel.

METHOD

1 Make the initial preparations and lay out the path (see Path basics, pages 10–12).

2 Set your string lines, before excavating all vegetation to a depth of at least 100 mm below the finished string line height. If preferred, cover the path area with polythene sheet.

3 Cut the stone edging to a width of 200 mm, and to lengths of 500 mm and 250 mm (see the box on Cutting stone, page 24).

4 Mix up enough mortar for bedding the border stones, using 3 parts sand to 1 part cement. Lay the sides of the path by bedding the stones firmly in mortar. Either leave a 20 mm gap between each piece of stone for mortar jointing (as for this path), or butt the stones together without a joint. Alternate the two sizes of stone along the path to add interest.

5 If you have left gaps, use a trowel to finish the joints with more of the same mortar mix. Use an old paint

4 Bed the stones along the sides of the path in mortar. Alternate the small and large pieces of stone.

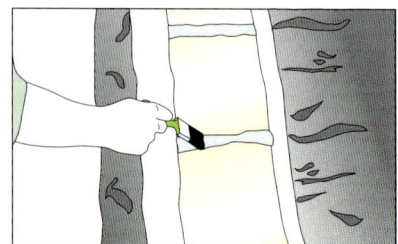

5 Fill gaps between the stones with mortar and smooth the surface with an old paint brush.

brush to smooth the surface of the mortar. Allow one or two days for it to dry.

6 Fill the area between the stone borders with gravel (approximately 50 mm deep), either matched to the colour of the stone or in contrasting, deeper shades. Rake the gravel in place and then tamp it until the surface is level and neat.

CLEANING STONE

If stone becomes stained and will not clean up with fresh water and a brush, add two cups of chlorine bleach to a bucket of water. Spread it over the surface with a broom and allow it to dry. The sun and chlorine will work to clean the surface of the stone.

Gravel is an inexpensive pathway material and is available in a variety of sizes and colours. This earth-coloured gravel teams beautifully with the cream-coloured stone running on one side and the brick wall on the other.

Edging styles

Paths often need to be contained and held in place by some sort of edging. Edges are needed to retain bedding sands and loose materials and to prevent bricks, blocks and stones from moving.

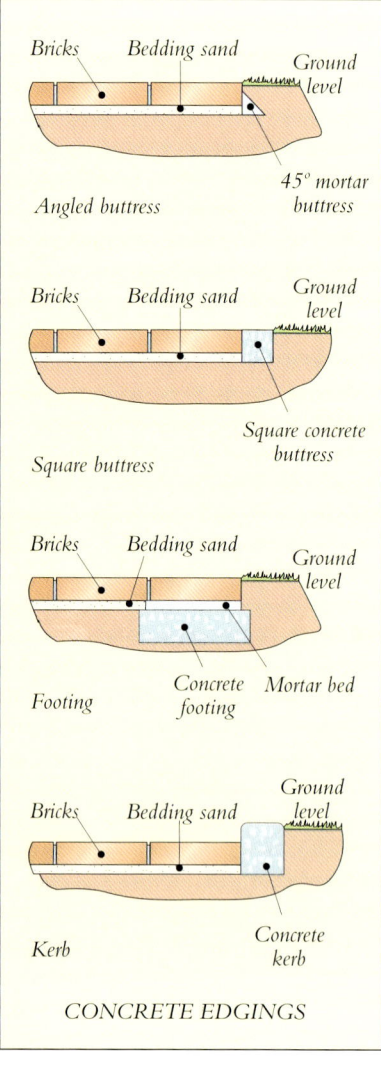

Angled buttress

45° mortar buttress

Square buttress

Square concrete buttress

Footing

Concrete footing *Mortar bed*

Kerb

Concrete kerb

CONCRETE EDGINGS

CONCRETE AND MORTAR EDGING FOR PATHS

Pavers, bricks and block paths need quite strong edges. Without them, the paving material will move and the bedding sand will wash out, causing the path to sink. Here are four ways of edging a path that will also make mowing easy.

● **Angled buttress**. After laying the path, cut away any loose material around the edge of the path down to the firm base. Trowel mortar (comprising 3 parts sand to 1 part cement) against the path edge at a 45 degree angle to form a buttress. Cover at least half the depth of the paving with mortar. An advantage of this sloping edge is that surrounding plants or lawn can grow up to the path edge, hiding the mortar.

● **Square buttress**. This is formed in a similar way to the previous edging, but the concrete creates a square-edged mower strip between the path and surrounding area. This remains visible, and many people do not choose to use it because of this. Also, formwork has to be set up to retain the concrete edging until it has set. However, the square buttress edging

The edge of the path can be designed to be a feature, depending on the contrast in materials or colours. These terracotta tiles add decoration as well as providing a line of separation between the path and the garden bed beside it.

does provide an easy way of maintaining neat edges on garden beds and lawn.

• **Concrete footing**. Like the angled buttress edging, the concrete footing is hidden from view but it is still able to retain the path. It is best to construct this type of edging before the path is laid. To do this, pour a strip of concrete, approximately 100 mm deep and 250 mm wide, beneath the edge bricks or blocks of the path. These are then mortared on to the concrete base and together they will contain the bedding sand and pathway material.

• **Concrete kerb**. This type of edging is used to redirect the flow of water and/or to retain an area that is higher than the path. It is best to construct the kerb before laying the path. Use 200 x 50 mm timber to form up both sides of the concrete strip, making it at least 100 mm wide, for strength. Fill this with concrete and level it with a float. Use an edging tool to round the corners on both sides. Allow to set for two to three days before removing the boards.

Precast concrete kerbs are also available in a variety of lengths and shapes from your local landscape supply centre.

BRICK EDGING

The edge bricks, blocks or pavers on a path are called the 'header' course. Header courses strengthen the edges of the paving because they are constructed using whole bricks, which fully contain the smaller cut sections. Header courses also add a decorative finish to the patterning of brick paving, because they can be laid in different patterns or colours for contrast. Practically, they can also make effective mower strips.

Header courses are laid on mortar with a concrete footing, or are held in place firmly by a buttress of square or 45 degree mortar. They can be laid in a choice of directions to contrast effectively with the paving. A square header course (or 'soldier' course) is laid at right angles to the path and a longitudinal header course is laid parallel to the path.

Raised brick edging is an alternative to header courses and acts as a kerb to retain garden beds or to direct the flow of water along the length of the path. Raised edge bricks can be laid in a variety of patterns for visual effect including saw-tooth, on-end or two–up–two–down (see the diagram below). Set these edge bricks in a mortar base and buttress them with additional side mortar to hold the bricks firmly in place.

TIMBER EDGING

Timber edging is suitable for retaining loose path materials such as bark and pebbles. Very durable hardwoods and pressure-impregnated softwoods are recommended for outside use. Lay these lengthways and fix in position using wooden pegs and galvanised nails. Peg spacing is usually every 1.2 m.

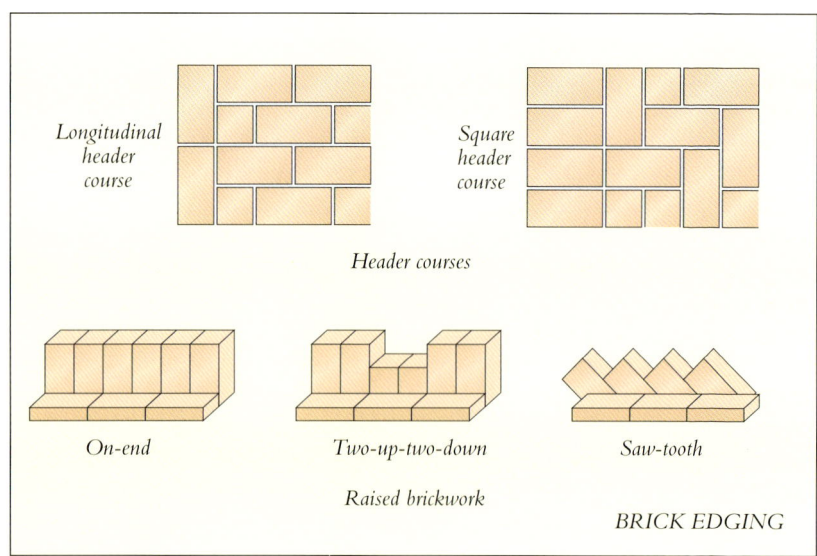

Longitudinal header course

Square header course

Header courses

On-end

Two-up-two-down

Saw-tooth

Raised brickwork

BRICK EDGING

ALTERNATIVE EDGINGS

Historical influences or the unavailability of materials in some areas have led to some innovative approaches in garden to path-edging techniques.

• Glass in the form of bottles, particularly the large, dark coloured beer or wine bottles, can be used as an edging and in retaining walls. To construct a bottle edge for your path, stand the bottles vertically upside down and push them into the soil. Set the finished height to a string line and support with a 45 degree or square buttress of mortar on one or both sides. Alternatively, lay the bottles horizontally and dry stack several layers. As you stack each layer, mortar only the neck parts of the bottles to hold them in place.

• Many Victorian and Edwardian paths and gardens were edged with loops of wire. Although they do little to support heavy path materials or to prevent erosion, they are excellent as a small, raised border. Today, these looped woven wire borders are available in rolls of galvanised wire, PVC-coated wire or powder-coated wire. Installation is easy: push the wire loops into the ground or, for permanency, incorporate them into your 45 degree buttress of mortar against the edge of a brick path.

Old railway sleepers are also good materials for edging, and they can be extended up into retaining walls or seating. Their weight is usually sufficient to hold them in place. Treated pine logs with pointed ends can be driven vertically into the ground to form raised edging, as can split logs. Purchase these in joined lengths or make them yourself and position them individually. They are particularly useful for curved paths.

TERRACOTTA TILES

Terracotta edging tiles add an old-world charm to the garden. They are used to separate the path from the garden beds, allowing the plants to spill over them. To hold the tiles upright, mortar them in position. If the path is constructed of a hard material such as brick, the tiles will be supported vertically on one side by the brick, but on the garden-bed side you will need to place a 45 degree supporting buttress of mortar.

STONE AND ROCK

Stone and rock are excellent forms of hard edging and they work equally well with paths of loose material, stepping stones and bricks. This material also works well in forming the edges for free-flowing and curved paths. To fix firmly into place, bed the stone or rock in 25–50 mm thick mortar. The gap between each stone can be mortared or left natural.

Steps

A change in level can create interest and give character to a garden. Steps are usually constructed to cope with a sloping site or to terrace a garden, and should be made from non-slip paving materials such as bricks, blocks, clay pavers, wood or stone.

PLANNING

If you are constructing steps there are a few considerations that will ensure that the finished result will be both functional and aesthetically pleasing.

• The incline of the steps should be gradual and the steps themselves should be as wide and inviting as possible. Narrow, steep steps can look daunting.

• The materials chosen to build the steps should match the garden setting and house architecture.

• Ascertain the degree of slope and then make a decision on the type of steps needed (see Coping with a slope, page 7).

• Work out the dimensions of the step. A comfortable step consists of a 150 mm riser and a tread length (front to back) of approximately 350 mm. The basic dimensions will vary, depending on the degree and length of slope as well as the materials used in construction. Risers should be vertical, but treads should have a 5–10 mm fall to the front to prevent water pooling, because this can make the step slippery and dangerous.

TYPES OF STEPS

• Single steps are best if they are wide and positioned for easy visibility, otherwise they may go unnoticed and cause people to trip. Place plants near them, or set lights in the garden to help bring them into view.

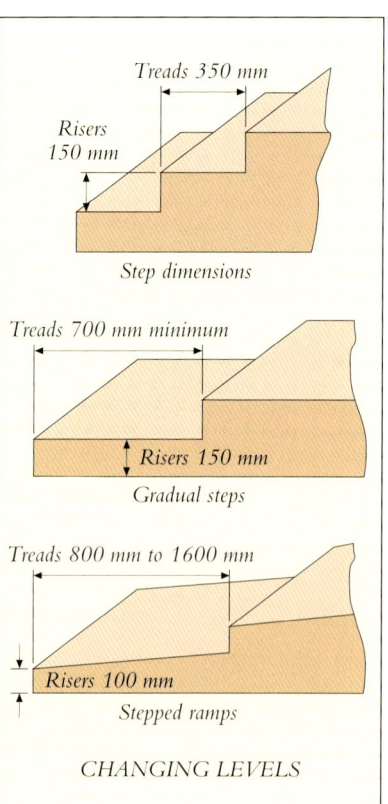

Treads 350 mm

Risers 150 mm

Step dimensions

Treads 700 mm minimum

Risers 150 mm

Gradual steps

Treads 800 mm to 1600 mm

Risers 100 mm

Stepped ramps

CHANGING LEVELS

These gently curving stone steps lead off a driveway up to a large, formal garden. The wide tread depth makes these steps safe and comfortable to use.

• Gradual steps laid on gentle inclines can have treads that are longer than normal, enabling the walker to step twice or more on the one tread. Another feature of gradually inclining paths is the inclusion of landings or rest areas, perhaps with a seat.

• Steep steps are necessary on sharply inclined ground. They have one-step treads and should be accompanied by a handrail for safety. The materials selected should be non-slip. If the flight of steps is lengthy, it may be better to terrace the area and to incorporate landings in the path. The landing could include a seat or some plantings to encourage the passerby to stop, rest or enjoy the view.

• Stepped ramps are appropriate on very long, gentle inclines. Risers remain vertical but the treads are not horizontal. For this to be an effective path, the risers should not be greater than 100 mm and treads should range from 800 mm to 1600 mm.

MATERIALS

Formal steps are usually constructed from materials such as bricks, pavers, stone, tiles, paving slabs or timber. Informal steps are generally constructed from materials such as railway sleepers, wood rounds, rock, logs, split stone or loose materials. Combination steps involve the use of both groups of materials, such as sleeper risers backed by brick treads.

Using informal materials is far less time consuming when constructing steps, and these are easily handled by the non-professional person. If you prefer to construct formal steps using tile or brick, you may need to seek professional assistance.

The following instructions show how to build three step types: a single brick step (see Brick or block path, page 18); a single sleeper step (see Brick and timber path, page 52); and a treated softwood step (see page 67).

METHOD FOR SINGLE BRICK STEP

1 Lay your path as far as possible until it becomes necessary to construct a step.

TOOLS

• Basic tool kit (see page 10)

MATERIALS

• Timber formwork

• Nails

• Concrete

• Bricks or clay pavers

---

2 Excavate a further distance of approximately 350–400 mm from the last row of bricks. This will create the space for the first step.

3 Using 150 x 50 mm timber, form up the front and side edges of this space to retain a concrete mix. The formwork should be positioned so that the start of the concrete will be at least 70 mm from the last row of bricks. Level the formwork before securing it with pegs and nailing it in position.

4 Mix and pour concrete to the top of the formwork, level and leave with a rough finish. Allow the concrete to dry for two to three days

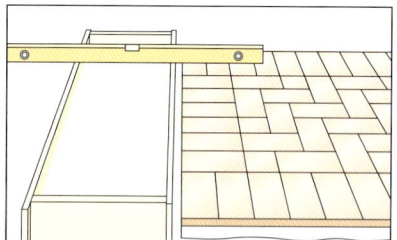

3 Form up the front and side edges for the step. Use a spirit level to check that the surface is level.

4 Pour the concrete into the formwork and level the surface with a float. Allow the concrete to dry.

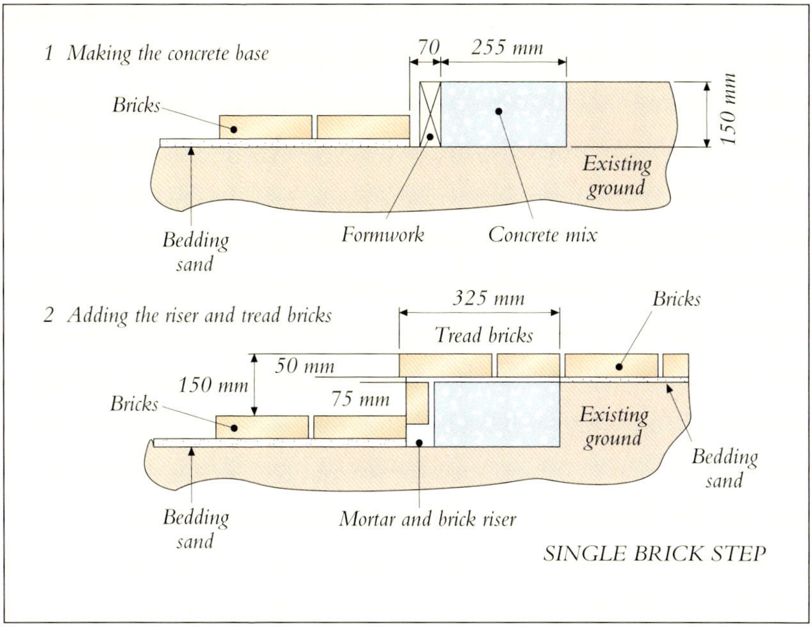

1 Making the concrete base

Bricks

70   255 mm

150 mm

Existing ground

Bedding sand

Formwork

Concrete mix

2 Adding the riser and tread bricks

325 mm

Tread bricks

Bricks

50 mm

150 mm

75 mm

Bricks

Existing ground

Bedding sand

Bedding sand

Mortar and brick riser

SINGLE BRICK STEP

before removing the formwork. (As an alternative to the concrete slab, consider using pre-cast concrete units or two courses of bricks.)

5 For this step, the risers are bricks laid on their side. Position the risers in the 70 mm gap left between the path and concrete. When mortaring them to the vertical face of the concrete, ensure that at least 75 mm of the riser is above the path. This will leave 25 mm of the riser brick sitting below the finished paving height, which will help to lock the riser into position. Once the tread bricks are in position, you will have achieved a step height of 150 mm.

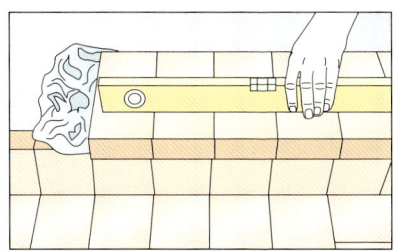

6 Mortar the tread bricks in place so that they overhang the riser bricks by 15–20 mm.

6 Mortar the tread bricks in position, ensuring that they have a slight fall of 5–10 mm to the front, and that they overhang the riser by 15–20 mm. Lay a second row of bricks running in the opposite direction to construct a tread of approximately 325 mm in depth.

7 Repeat this procedure to create another step, or continue the path.

This step is constructed using a single sleeper, which functions as both the tread and riser for the step.

TOOLS

- Basic tool kit (see page 10)

MATERIALS

- Old railway sleepers (see Brick and timber path, page 52)
- 75 mm (3 in) lost-head, galvanised nails

METHOD FOR THE SINGLE SLEEPER STEP

1 Lay the path as far as possible at one level (see page 52) until it becomes necessary to build a step.

2 Place the edges of the railway sleepers on top of the existing edges (running along the length of the path). Overlap the edges of the sleepers by at least 300 mm and fix by skew-nailing with 75 mm (3 in) twisted, galvanised nails (see step 5, pages 52–3). The position of the step should start at the back edge of the last bay of paving to keep the pattern of your path continuous.

3 Cut the riser and tread sleeper to the same width as the path and place it between the two edge sleepers. Fix by skew-nailing. The thickness of the sleepers will determine the height of the step.

4 To continue the path, create further bays, screeding off and laying the bricks so that your path will continue. Incorporate more steps along the path where needed.

2 Place the edges of the sleepers for the next level along the path so they overlap the existing sleepers.

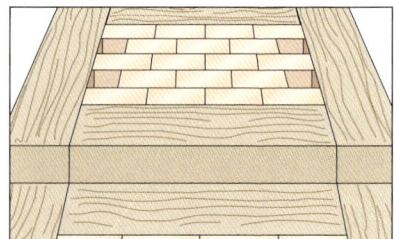

4 With the sleepers in place, continue the path by creating bays of bricks surrounded by sleepers.

METHOD FOR THE TREATED SOFTWOOD STEP

TOOLS

- Basic tool kit (page 10)
- Circular saw or panel saw
- Sander

MATERIALS

- Three 150 x 50 x 300 mm preservative-treated softwood (joists)
- Seven 100 x 25 x 950 mm preservative-treated softwood decking
- 50 mm (2 in) twisted, flat-head, galvanised nails

A single step made from treated softwood is very easy to construct and will weather well.

1 Cut the treated softwood for the three joists to a length of 300 mm. Re-treat any cut surfaces.

2 Cut the lengths of softwood decking to 950 mm.

3 To make the frame for the step, nail two lengths of softwood decking to the three joists, one length for the front of the step, and one for the back. Use two flat-head nails at each attachment point.

4 Nail four lengths of softwood decking on top of the joists to create the tread. Allow for a 10 mm overhang on both the front and back of the step.

5 To complete the step, cut the remaining 950 mm length of decking in half lengthways. Attach the two halves to the base of the step, one piece at the front, and one piece at the back.

6 Lightly sand all edges. Leave natural, paint or stain, as desired. Place or fix the step in position.

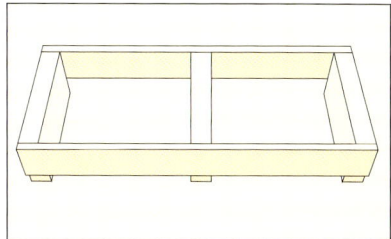

3 To make the basic frame for the step, nail the front and back lengths of decking to the three joists.

Path repair

Paths made of natural materials weather well with time and look wonderful in the garden, but they do require some maintenance and repairs from time to time. Damage can occur as a result of the presence of large trees or from erosion. Some common problems such as tree root damage and sinkage can be overcome through a few different solutions.

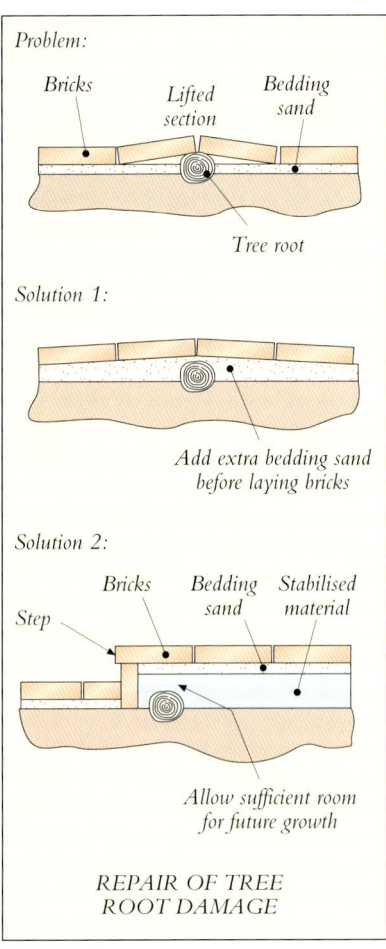

Problem:

Bricks — Lifted section — Bedding sand

Tree root

Solution 1:

Add extra bedding sand before laying bricks

Solution 2:

Step — Bricks — Bedding sand — Stabilised material

Allow sufficient room for future growth

REPAIR OF TREE
ROOT DAMAGE

TREE ROOT DAMAGE

Probably the most common cause of damage to paths in the garden is uplifting or cracking by tree roots. This damage usually occurs over a long period of time, and it is only when a brick or section of path begins to jut dangerously above the surrounding area that we realise repairs are needed. If this early sign is ignored, the damage will increase with whole sections of the path cracking and lifting. By the time such severe damage has occurred, the offending tree is usually quite well-established and its removal is difficult.

If the tree cannot be relocated or if you cannot re-direct the path to go around it, consult a qualified tree surgeon as to whether it would be adversely affected by root pruning. In most cases, however, the path can be repaired by following one of two simple methods.

If you cannot repair or redirect the path, probably the only solution will be to try to hide the damage with pots, furniture or ornaments.

For your path to stay an attractive and safe feature of your garden, it may need occasional maintenance. Tree roots may cause damage, or the path may become mouldy and slippery if it is not cleaned regularly (see page 43).

RAMP THE PATH

If the damage occurs in a small section of a long length of path, it is possible to create a slight undulation over the problem area. This disguises the problem and maintains the existing level and direction of the path. To minimise the effect of the undulation, lift the bricks in the damaged section of the path, plus several metres on either side. Add extra bedding sand to create a gradual ramp up and over the tree root.

Screed the path and lay the new area (see pages 11–17).

REDIRECT THE PATH

If you have sufficient space in your garden, incorporate a curve into your path to redirect it around the troubled area. Lift the path materials and remove and replace any broken or cracked pavers, bricks, tiles or stone. Form up and lay the path again (see Laying the path, pages 14–17).

STEP THE PATH

If the path is already ramped on an incline, it may be appropriate to create a step or landing over the root. This will leave ample room for future growth. However, if your path is on level ground, stepping your path will mean that the surrounding area should be raised. For this you will need to add compacted fill beneath the new level of path before screeding and laying the path again. For further information on step construction see Steps, pages 62–7.

REPAIRING UNEVEN SECTIONS

Uneven sections appear in paths due to small sinkages in the base material.

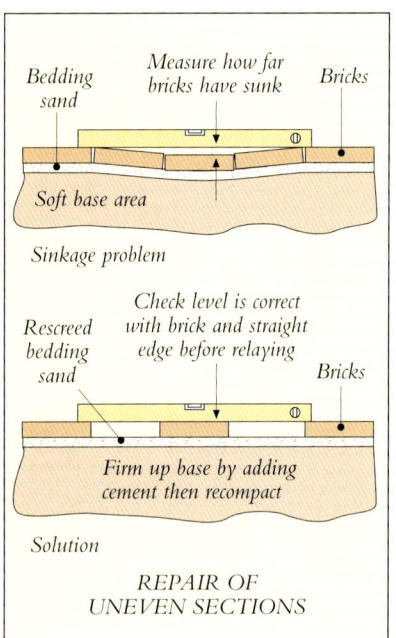

Bedding sand

Measure how far bricks have sunk

Bricks

Soft base area

Sinkage problem

Rescreed bedding sand

Check level is correct with brick and straight edge before relaying

Bricks

Firm up base by adding cement then recompact

Solution

REPAIR OF UNEVEN SECTIONS

This can occur as a result of excess water flowing under the path from broken drainage pipes or because of poor compaction of the original base layer during construction. To repair any area of sinkage in a path carry out the following steps.

METHOD

1 Place a spirit level over the path to determine the affected area.

2 Lift the surface layer of the sunk pathway materials.

3 If the sinkage is small, add extra bedding sand, and then screed the area with a straight-edge or spirit level (see Screeding, pages 12–13). If the sinkage is large, remove sand and add more base material. Sprinkle dry cement over the surface and rake it through the base thoroughly. Compact the base materials and hose the surface lightly so that the cement will set, hardening the base and preventing further sinkage. Screed and level the path.

4 To check that the surface is level, place a brick in the centre of the re-screeded area. Place a straight-edge across the path from side to side, touching the centre brick. If the centre brick is below the straight-edge, add more sand. If the straight-edge rocks on the centre brick, take some sand out.

5 Lay the pathway materials again to match the original pattern.

Tools for building paths

Some of the most useful tools for constructing paths are shown below. Build up your tool kit gradually. Most of the tools can be purchased from your local hardware store.

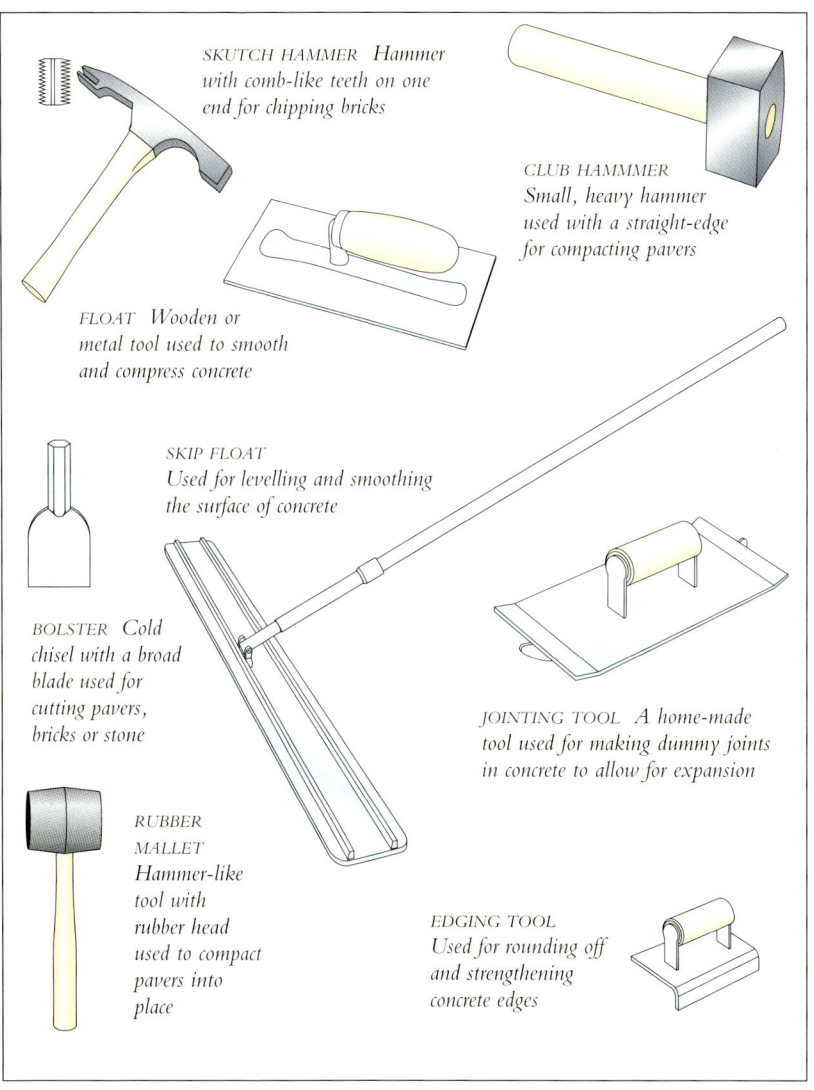

SKUTCH HAMMER *Hammer with comb-like teeth on one end for chipping bricks*

CLUB HAMMMER *Small, heavy hammer used with a straight-edge for compacting pavers*

FLOAT *Wooden or metal tool used to smooth and compress concrete*

SKIP FLOAT *Used for levelling and smoothing the surface of concrete*

BOLSTER *Cold chisel with a broad blade used for cutting pavers, bricks or stone*

JOINTING TOOL *A home-made tool used for making dummy joints in concrete to allow for expansion*

RUBBER MALLET *Hammer-like tool with rubber head used to compact pavers into place*

EDGING TOOL *Used for rounding off and strengthening concrete edges*

Index